Pra...

Diversity Playbook

"I sincerely enjoyed reading this book; it was very engaging. This book challenged me, encouraged me, and also gave me a rich biblical foundation and historical view into our African American heritage. This book gave valuable tools, prayers, and insights on how to use proven strategies and lessons learned in the area of diversity, equity, and inclusion for faith-based nonprofit organizations. I certainly plan to use this book as a helpful guide as we continue our journey in D, E, & I."

—**Vicki Harris,** Sr. Vice President of Global Human Resources and D, E, & I for Our Daily Bread Ministries, a worldwide organization located in 38 countries

"Christian organizations are increasingly working toward diversity, equity, and inclusion. With *Diversity Playbook*, Michelle L. and Michelle W., two wise and experienced experts, effectively equip and empower readers to lead this shift. This resource is brilliantly written, boldly honest, and biblical. Focusing on shalom, koinonia, and reconciliation, this playbook is an essential read for *all* Christian organizations."

—**Rev. Emmett G. Price III,** PhD, President & CEO, Black Christian Experience Resource Center

"*Diversity Playbook* is full of practical wisdom for diversity professionals, allies, and organizations looking to transform their institutions into places that increasingly resemble biblical, beloved community. This playbook is the collective guidance of two women who have committed decades of their lives to doing the work of justice as diversity professionals within Christian organizations. Christian institutions have for decades been challenged with working toward the biblical calls to reconciliation and justice. The authors of this volume share their expertise with readers on how to achieve these seemingly intangible goals through exploring both what individuals and organizations can do to create systemic change. Uniquely, this book has content for three important constituencies in this regard: individual diversity professionals, their allies and supporters, as well as leaders of Christian organizations looking to make biblical justice something permanent in their institution through strategic, systemic change. Readers who want more than descriptions of social problems and theories about advancing the work of justice will be pleasantly surprised by this slim volume containing lifetimes of wisdom on how to pragmatically work toward change."

—**Eric Nykamp,** LMSW, Producer of the Antioch Podcast: *Conversations About Biblical Antiracism*

"Powerful and timely, *Diversity Playbook* equips leaders, allies, and outliers as Christ's agents of healing. A roadmap to human flourishing, diverse communities are God's ideal where holy restoration and love defeat hatred, division, and brokenness. A crucial book for such a time as this!"

—**Mimi Haddad,** PhD, President, CBE International

"For some people, diversity is a way to be 'in' or politically correct. But following the biblical mandates, Loyd-Paige and Williams demonstrate that diversity and difference are at the heart of Christ's Kingdom. *Diversity Playbook* is personal, practical, prophetic, and filled with loads of wisdom. It is an indispensable tool for diversity professionals and a broad array of leaders in Christian institutions, organizations, and churches."

—**Dennis Hollinger,** PhD, President Emeritus & Senior Distinguished Professor of Christian Ethics, Gordon-Conwell Theological Seminary

DIVERSITY PLAYBOOK

FOREWORD BY BRENDA SALTER-MCNEIL

DIVERSITY PLAYBOOK

Recommendations and
Guidance for Christian
Organizations

MICHELLE R. LOYD-PAIGE & **MICHELLE D. WILLIAMS**

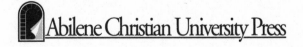

Abilene Christian University Press

DIVERSITY PLAYBOOK
Recommendations and Guidance for Christian Organizations

LIBRARY OF CONGRESS CATALOGING-IN-PUBLICATION DATA
Names: Loyd-Paige, Michelle, author. | Williams, Michelle D., 1974- author.
Title: The diversity playbook : recommendations and guidance for Christian organizations /
    Michelle Loyd-Paige and Michelle D. Williams.
Description: Abilene, Texas : Abilene Christian University Press, 2021. | Includes bibliographical references.
Identifiers: LCCN 2021012908 (print) | LCCN 2021012909 (ebook) | ISBN 9781684263714 (trade paperback) |
    ISBN 9781684269129 (ebook)
Subjects: LCSH: Christianity and culture. | Cultural pluralism—Religious aspects—Christianity. |
    Diversity in the workplace. | Religious institutions. | Work environment. | Race relations—
    Religious aspects—Christianity.
Classification: LCC BR115.C8 L69 2021 (print) | LCC BR115.C8 (ebook) | DDC 261—dc23
LC record available at https://lccn.loc.gov/2021012908
LC ebook record available at https://lccn.loc.gov/2021012909

Cover design by ThinkPen Design | Interior text design by Strong Design, Sandy Armstrong

For information contact:
Abilene Christian University Press, ACU Box 29138, Abilene, Texas 79699

1-877-816-4455 | www.acupressbooks.com

21 22 23 24 25 26 / 7 6 5 4 3 2 1

CONTENTS

ACKNOWLEDGMENTS

We would both like to thank the person who brought us together many years ago, the Rev. Dr. Brenda Salter-McNeil. You paved the way for us to be diversity professionals in Christian higher education. You have been a mentor, encourager, and prayer partner. Thank you.

I (Michelle L.) would like to thank my friend and coauthor, Michelle Williams, for being the catalyst for turning playful banter about writing into a reality. I don't know if I would have done this without you. I also want to give a shout-out to all the young diversity professionals who have job-shadowed me over the years. Your commitment to this work and fresh ideas give me hope for the future. A thank you to Reggie, Libby, Susie, and Eric. Thank you for the space to laugh, cry, and grow. And finally, a shout-out to my husband: thanks for your encouragement and steady supply of baked goods throughout this project.

I (Michelle W.) would like to thank the amazingly talented and multifaceted Dr. Michelle Loyd-Paige. Your tireless energy is inspiring. Thank you for lending your voice and years of experience to our project. To the mentors who recognized potential in me before I saw it in myself (Barry Hall, Brent Baker, and Ruth White), thank you. To the students who challenged me, taught me, and listened to me, thank you. To my dad, Ronald Otis Williams, who passed on his gift of writing, I am indebted. Finally, to my mom and stepdad, Howard and Casenia Stripling, without whom this wouldn't have been possible, thanks for letting me share your space during my sabbatical!

FOREWORD

I got up to speak right after the president of Georgetown University humbly told the powerful story of how his academic institution intentionally worked to address its racist past. He explained how a collection of Georgetown professors, students, alumni, and genealogists uncovered the dark history of how the nation's most prominent Jesuit priests, who ran the school in 1838, owned two hundred seventy-two enslaved African men, women, and children. These human beings were sold to help secure the future of this Catholic academic institution that is known today as Georgetown University.

In response, the students at Georgetown voted to increase their tuition to benefit descendants of the two hundred seventy-two enslaved Africans whom the Jesuits sold to build their academic institution. Together with the board of directors, administrators, and faculty, they courageously confronted the wrenching question of "What is owed to the descendants of slaves who were sold to help ensure the college's survival?" Their answer was decided in a groundbreaking vote to create a fund, which was a remarkable instance of reparations for slavery by any prominent American institution.

I was so inspired by what I had just heard that I began my message to the presidents of Christian colleges and universities gathered at this conference with a question of my own. I asked, "Are you ready to journey toward a systemic shift in the reconciliation work taking place on your campus?" I asked this question because I have witnessed the burden for the many people hired to serve as diversity professionals within Christian organizations who fail. Over the course of my years as a consultant to many Christian organizations, I have seen an alarming trend of turnover; and when diversity professionals leave, they often feel isolated and defeated. These dedicated Christians, who are often people of color, are unsuccessful because they have not been adequately equipped or empowered to lead systemic change. It is this type of guidance and insight that is needed to genuinely produce diversity, equity, and inclusion on Christian college and university campuses and in Christian organizations as a whole.

In the Gospel of Mark 2:21–22, Jesus said,

> No one sews a patch of unshrunk cloth on an old garment. Otherwise, the new piece will pull away from the old, making the tear worse. And no one pours new wine into old wineskins. Otherwise, the wine will burst the skins, and both the wine and the wineskins will be ruined. No, they pour new wine into new wineskins.

I believe this text is an urgent, biblical call for a major paradigm shift in Christian communities. This is especially true in the way Christian organizations are approaching the work of racial, ethnic, gender, and cultural diversity. As Christians, we must move away from simply adding diversity to actually making cross-cultural friendships to recover the systemic realities of justice, advocacy, and power that biblical reconciliation was always meant to address. This is nonnegotiable for those who want to achieve true, healthy diversity and racial justice in their institutions and organizations. That's why we need a new way to reimagine reconciliation, diversity, and the vitally important role of the person charged with leading this work in their organization or institution.

Diversity professionals and Christian organizations need a new way forward if they are going to stay on this journey and be successful in this work. No one knows that better than the authors of this book do. In my thirty years of experience working with Christian institutions and organizations, Michelle Loyd-Paige and Michelle Williams are two of the finest, most well informed, and interculturally competent diversity professionals I have known. Their years of experience and leadership at many levels within systemic hierarchies have allowed them to learn valuable lessons and best practices that have enabled them to stand the test of time. Now they are making all the wisdom, experience, and expertise they have learned over the years available to everyone in this much-needed resource.

I am grateful that these two seasoned diversity professionals have proposed a new wineskin and antiracist approach that will enable others to move beyond just focusing on relationship building and numerical diversity to actually repairing broken systems and engaging power dynamics. I pray that as you read this book, it will equip you to build communities of reconciliation that produce personal transformation and systemic change from a Christian perspective. So now, the future of reconciliation at your college, university, or organization is in your hands—literally! Use it well, and I hope you will see true reconciliation and diversity become more of a reality in your sphere of influence so that all people can reach their full, God-given potential.

Rev. Dr. Brenda Salter-McNeil

INTRODUCTION

> *Where there is no guidance the people fall, but in abundance of counselors there is victory.*
> —**Proverbs 11:14** NASB

We were in Chicago. It was 2010 and we were gathered with Dr. Brenda Salter-McNeil and three other diversity professionals. Some were brand new to the profession and some had years of experience under their belts. But everyone in this small, invited group had committed to meet quarterly for a year. We all felt isolated in our organizations and were looking for both encouragement and best-practice ideas. Since that time, we two have come in and out of each other's lives to share successes, frustrations, pain points, resources, and "Girl, we should write a book with all we've been through!" Just over a decade later, here we are—writing a book. What started out as a pipe dream has become a reality.

From the time we first dreamed about writing a book until now, diversity has become a buzz word within Christian organizations. Although most of our experience has been within Christian higher education, we have both been consultants for and associated with various Christian organizations. By "Christian organizations" we mean churches, nonprofits, parachurch organizations, and institutions of higher learning (Christian colleges/universities and seminaries). Through networks, associates, professional organizations, and our own experience, we've seen Christian organizations struggle with diversity as a concept and in praxis. More importantly, we've seen and felt the fallout that occurs when these organizations neglect addressing their racialized systems.

Diversity within Christian Institutions of Higher Learning

In 2017, Pete Mejaras wrote about the changes he had witnessed in Christian higher education in his introductory chapter to the edited volume *Diversity Matters: Race, Ethnicity, and the Future of Christian Higher Education*. In his chapter, Mejaras described the significant demographic shift that has happened within the racial and ethnic composition among undergraduate students attending the member institutions of the Coalition of Christian Colleges and Universities (CCCU). Student populations have become less White. To a lesser degree, the racial and ethnic composition of faculty in Christian higher education has also become less White. The two charts below provide a snapshot of changes in compositional diversity from 2008 to 2019, a decade of change. The numbers are taken from IPEDS (Integrated Post-Secondary Education Data System). Chart A represents students and Chart B represents faculty.

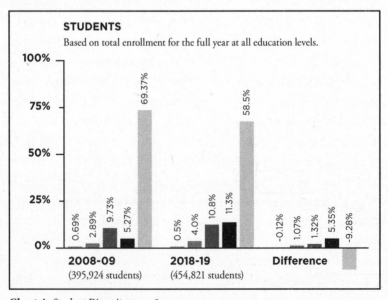

Chart A. Student Diversity—2008–19

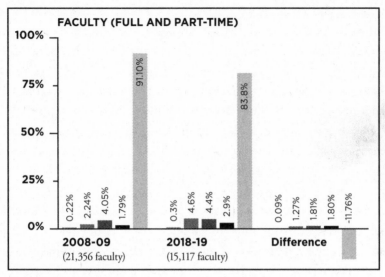

FACULTY (FULL AND PART-TIME)

	2008-09 (21,356 faculty)	2018-19 (15,117 faculty)	Difference
American Indian or Alaska Native	0.22%	0.3%	0.09%
Asian/Native Hawaiian or Other Pacific Islander	2.24%	4.6%	1.27%
Black/African American	4.05%	4.4%	1.81%
Hispanic/Latino	1.79%	2.9%	1.80%
White	91.10%	83.8%	-11.76%

Chart B. Faculty Diversity—2008–19

- American Indian or Alaska Native
- Asian/Native Hawaiian or Other Pacific Islander
- Black/African American
- Hispanic/Latino
- White

What is not indicated in the charts above is the fact that nearly half of all CCCU schools have diverse (nonwhite and noninternational) student populations greater than 30 percent, at least nine CCCU institutions have student-of-color populations over 40 percent, four have student-of-color populations over 60 percent, and one, Nyack College, has a student-of-color population of over 80 percent. From 2004 to 2019, there has been a 14 percent increase in the number of students of color attending CCCU schools. White faculty and administrators account for just over 90 percent in 2009 and just over 83 percent in 2019. The diverse student populations on Christian campuses are growing faster than the number of diverse faculty and staff. What the tables above do not demonstrate is that the number of diversity professionals has not kept pace with the increasingly more diverse student body and the growing calls for more welcoming and inclusive campuses. Furthermore, the charts do not tell the story of the number of diversity professionals who have walked away from Christian higher education (going to the corporate sector to lead diversity efforts or just leaving diversity work all together) because of the challenges associated with leading diversity efforts during a season of two pandemics—COVID-19 and the rise of White nationalism.

Christian seminaries are not exempt from this issue. In fact, according to the Association for Theological Schools (ATS), the trend of increasing student diversity but stagnant faculty/staff representation is consistent with their undergraduate counterparts in these numbers as well (see Annual Data 2018–2019, comparison of composition of faculty and racial/ethnic enrollment data).[1] From our vantage point, both seminaries that are affiliated with denominations and seminaries that are not affiliated with a denomination have struggled to recruit and retain diverse faculty. Both have struggled with how to equip their students—future leaders of the church—with the tools they will need to address the "browning" of the church and the polarization found within the church on issues of race, gender, sexual orientation, social justice, and critical race theory. But it is not just the equipping of future leaders of the church that is being asked of seminaries; current pastors and leaders are also asking for help on how to navigate difficult conversations, hard truths, and wounded congregants. Seminaries with resources are scrambling to equip and position themselves to meet this growing need. Seminaries without the resources are wondering where to start, and this playbook provides initial guidance.

Diversity within Nonprofits, Churches, and Parachurch Ministries

Over the last few years, we've seen several prominent Christian organizations publicly falter because of their mishandling of diversity matters. *Relevant Magazine* went through a very public process that resulted in their CEO, Cameron Strange, stepping down from his post. Former employee Andre Henry wrote a heart-wrenching article on *Medium.com* regarding the toxic culture within this organization.

---

[1] "2018–2019 Annual Data Tables," https://www.ats.edu/uploads/resources/institutional -data/annual-data-tables/2018-2019-annual-data-tables.pdf.

In the spring of 2019, theologian Ekemini Uwan spoke at the 2019 Sparrow Women conference. Conference attendees walked out during her session and the organization decided not to post her video because of the public discomfort. The organization apologized for mishandling the fallout from Ekemini's keynote speech, in which she addressed issues surrounding "Whiteness." However, the damage was done.

In 2021, a Washington Post headline shouted: "Newly leaked letter details allegations that Southern Baptist leaders mishandled sex abuse claims." The allegations of brought by several women state that some of the women were bullied and that leaders were resistant to initiating any kind of reforms in handling allegations of sexual abuse.[2] Furthermore, several Black pastors made public their exit from the Southern Baptist Convention, citing an SBC November 30, 2020, statement on race (which did not include any Black authors) that took aim at Critical Race Theory. Among other things, the presidents who wrote the statement said, "It is dangerous to view humans and conflict primarily through the lens of race or gender or sexuality instead of via scriptural concepts such as sin."[3] If the denominations we are affiliated with had made such a statement in the aftermath of the killing of George Floyd, Breonna Taylor, and so many more, we could not in good conscious remain as members of that denomination. Why? Because that denomination doesn't see systemic racism or systemic sexism as something the church should address. And because it would be a clear signal to us that the only remedy the church saw was prayer. Don't get us wrong, prayer is a beautiful and needed thing. But prayer alone is not enough. The Bible says faith without works is dead (James 2:14–26).

The above paragraphs mention incidents that were made public. However, having spent countless hours with colleagues, friends, leaders, and clients, we know that ignorant, hurtful, and blatantly racist/sexist

---

[2] Sarah Pulliam Bailey, "Newly Leaked Letter Details Allegations That Southern Baptist Leaders Mishandled Sex Abuse Claims," *Washington Post*, June 5, 2021, www.washingtonpost.com/religion/2021/06/05/russell-moore-southern-baptist-sex-abuse-allegations/.

[3] Sarah Pulliam Bailey and Michelle Boorstein, "Several Black Pastors Break with the Southern Baptist Convention over a Statement on Race," *Washington Post*, December 23, 2020, www.washingtonpost.com/religion/2020/12/23/black-pastors-break-southern-baptist-critical-race-theory/.

comments and incidents occur every day within Christian organizations. This heart-wrenching fact has existed for quite some time. Prior to the election of President Donald Trump, polarization around race existed. However, with his election it has moved into toxic polarization. After the election, there seemed to be an increase in intolerance toward diversity, a resurgence of racist incidents, and a rise in White nationalism even within Christian organizations.

With the election of Trump, evangelicals have struggled with identity issues. We use the term *evangelical* because the public discourse has surrounded this particular group of Christians as supporters of the president and his policies. In 2016, the Pew Research Center reported that 81 percent of White evangelicals voted for Trump;[4] and in 2020, 78 percent of White evangelicals voted for Trump.[5] In both presidential elections, evangelicals of color adamantly opposed Trump's election and administration. In fact, in 2020, 90 percent of Black protestants voted for Joseph Biden. Ninety percent. This deep divide between White evangelicals and evangelicals (and protestants) of color continues to grow as conversations about same-sex marriage, White supremacy, critical race theory, the place of women in the church and as leaders, immigration, and police reform have become politicized and polarizing. As conversations (if you can call them that) become the topic of sermons, statements by individual churches, and positions of denominations, it is no wonder that members are leaving the church and denominations are splitting. While there is a general "head nod" or mental assent to the need to diversify our churches, nonprofits, parachurch ministries, seminaries, and schools, the reality is that deep divides still exist. Many Christian organizations have sought to recruit, add, or develop diversity professionals from within to address issues of intolerance, discrimination, and injustice that have been uncovered within their organizations. These issues are reflective of not only a history of discrimination and oppression in the United States but also the

---

[4] Jessica Martínez and Gregory A. Smith, "How the Faithful Voted: A Preliminary 2016 Analysis," Pew Research Center, November 9, 2016, www.pewresearch.org/fact-tank/2016/11/09/how-the-faithful-voted-a-preliminary-2016-analysis/.

[5] Gregory A. Smith, "White Christians Continue to Favor Trump over Biden, but Support Has Slipped," Pew Research Center, October 13, 2020, www.pewresearch.org/fact-tank/2020/10/13/white-christians-continue-to-favor-trump-over-biden-but-support-has-slipped/.

current social and political climate of incivility and intolerance. Hence, the need for this playbook.

Diversity Matters to God

The definition of *diversity* is fairly simple. Sociologically speaking, it means "difference." When referring to humans, it includes all the various social categories individuals can belong to as a result of their social identities—race, class, gender, faith tradition, sexual orientation, political party affiliation, and so on. However, while the definition of *diversity* is fairly simple, its meaning is complex. For some, diversity is something to pursue and celebrate. Diversity is an added value. It means opportunities to learn from and about others. It means we are better together than we are apart. It is a gift from God.

However, for others the thought of pursuing diversity is frightening—as frightening as the monster hiding underneath the bed of a child who is afraid of the dark. Diversity is to be feared because it means embracing difference, and some differences, for these individuals, are too great to bridge. Diversity is frightening when it means compromising what one holds as true, such as with the belief that working alongside nonbelievers is to affirm that their nonbelief is a valid position.

The position we take in this guidebook is that diversity is something to be pursued and celebrated. Granted, the pursuit of diversity is messy work, but it is good work. Study after study has demonstrated the educational benefits of the presence of diversity in higher education, in a democratic society, and in the business sector. Diversity is not something that is coming; diversity is already here. We see it in the latest census reports and population forecasts. The proportion of those identifying solely as White is decreasing. The fasted growing churches around the world are ethnic churches. But value of diversity is more than just reflecting the demographic changes to national and global populations—you can have diversity in numbers but have a toxic environment and not reap the benefits of diversity. When diversity is pursued, celebrated, and leveraged, the benefits of diversity become evident. What are they? Well, while not direct correlations—that is the larger the number of diverse people, the greater the number of benefits—what has generally been found is that there are fewer feelings of isolation for marginalized populations, there is more creativity across teams, people are better prepared to work with local neighbors and on a global stage, there are across-the-board higher levels of academic achievement for all students, businesses experience higher levels of productivity from their employees, and there is an improvement of near- and long-term intergroup relations.

Our commitment to diversity in Christian organizations comes from our firm belief that diversity matters to God—and that if it matters to God, then it should matter to us. If it is a gift to us from God, then we should not be afraid of it, because every gift from God is a good gift.

Theologically we understand that diversity was God's intent from the beginning of creation. God created diverse animals, plants, light sources, land masses, bodies of water, and human beings. The male and female creation were made in the image of the diverse and triune God. God instructed Noah to make sure to have two of each kind on the ark to ensure repopulation of diverse creatures.

Throughout the biblical narrative we see God's celebration of diversity. The Old Testament prophets continually demanded justice and equity for the diverse "others" who occupied the land with the children of Israel. While there are varying opinions on God's intended outcome for the Tower of Babel, we see God intentionally scattering humankind so they could continue populating diverse lands and developing diverse cultures. We understand that the people built the tower out of pride and that the Lord gave the people different languages so that they could not understand one another (see Gen. 11:6–9); nevertheless, we also see at work a celebration of diversity. God could have simply destroyed the people, but God did not. God could have allowed them to speak the same language and just scattered them. God did not. Rather, God allowed them to live. God scattered them and sent them to inhabit new lands and to either develop or enhance other cultures based on their new geographic locations.

The ministry of Jesus highlighted the inclusion of all gifts—from the women who walked with him and supported his ministry to the encounter with the Samaritan woman. From his welcome of children to his advocacy for the poor and powerless, we see Jesus embracing and including all persons in his reconciliation quest. At the Pentecost event, we witness the power of the Holy Spirit across barriers of language, tribe, ethnicity, and nationality. People heard others speaking in their native languages. Out of this beautiful celebration of diversity the church was birthed. Finally, we see the awe-inspiring vision of Revelation, depicting a great multitude from every tribe, nation, people, and language in white robes standing before the throne of God. The thread of diversity runs throughout Scripture. It is intentional and divine.

Understanding diversity as divine frees us up to relegate diversity work to God. We will say this repeatedly throughout this book. It is fundamental to our survival as Christian diversity professionals. It is also what separates us from secular diversity professionals. We put our assurance and our hope for more diverse, inclusive, and welcoming organizations into the hands of a God who desires this more than we do. We trust that our labor is not in vain because diversity work is kingdom work. This means it is under the rulership of God. Daily submitting your work to God's rule and reign because it *belongs to God* changes your perception of diversity work in significant ways.

Our Context

The two of us have a cumulative total of over forty years in Christian higher education and consulting with Christian organizations. With regard to our higher education experience, we have witnessed our respective institutions increase in student diversity and wrestle with how to best serve them. We each have been involved in diversity-related leadership roles. Michelle W. began as a seminary student at the institution where she was hired as multicultural director, and she then transitioned into the director of the cultural center on campus. She retained these roles and added a student affairs title that led to greater leadership with majority culture students. Moving cross-country, she took a position as dean of students for a global seminary, which allowed her to have greater control over the programmatic and institutional resources allocated for diversity.

Michelle L. began as a sociology professor at a Christian university more than thirty years ago. As a professor, she focused on diversity and inclusion. After leaving the classroom, she spent nine years as an academic diversity program dean and became an executive-level chief diversity officer.

Around 2015, she began consulting with various Christian organizations and nonprofits.

With regard to higher education, we have each launched new programs on our respective campuses, helped to manage diversity incidents, been the representation and spokespeople for diversity within our communities, created safe spaces for students to share concerns, and been advisors to faculty and senior leadership. With regard to our consulting work, we have been invited to work with for-profit and nonprofit faith-based organizations because of our work in Christian higher education. In many ways, the concerns and the work are the same. For the most part, both are looking to more closely resemble the kingdom of God in both composition and interaction. But in some ways, these types of organizations, while having similar faith-based values and longings for more compositional diversity, have differing opportunities and challenges.

Both of us have been engaged in the work of the local church for more than thirty years. Michelle W. served as a youth pastor and associate pastor at a multiethnic church in Glenpool, Oklahoma, for seven years. Michelle L. has served as the associate pastor in two Black churches, currently serves in a multiracial, justice-proclaiming church, and has launched her own multiethnic women's ministry. These pastoral ministry roles exposed some of the challenges of cross-cultural communications in worship and leadership styles. Church ministry is unique in that pastors/leaders are expected to feed and nurture the sheep regardless of racial/ethnic identity.

Again, the overwhelming diversity clashes revolve around cultural expectations and norms. Generally, denominations play a huge role in shaping church culture and polity. Countless conversations, workshops, venting sessions, and consulting calls lead us to believe that denominational multiethnic ministry directors/pastors face similar challenges to the ones we face as diversity leaders within higher education, nonprofits, and parachurch organizations.

Over the years, we have watched the number of diversity professionals in Christian organizations grow. However, many have felt overwhelmed by the tasks presented to them and have left after only a few years. New diversity professionals may have any number of job titles, including but not limited to multicultural student program director; Act Six program director; international student advisor; diversity admissions specialist; dean of intercultural students; diversity committee chair; pastor for diversity and reconciliation; associate pastor for community and culture building; chief diversity officer; special assistant to the president; vice-president for diversity, equity, and inclusion; and multiethnic ministries director or pastor. Job titles may vary, but the challenges to advancing diversity and inclusion are often the same.

Why a Diversity Playbook?

To the diversity professionals, stories of disturbing incidents and burnout may be familiar to you (and perhaps even an expectation). We are sure you have your own version of horrific and painful incidents that shine a light on the hidden crevices of systemic and individual racism within your organizations. For you seasoned professionals, we hope this book will affirm some of the responses and strategies you've begun to implement. We hope you have moments when our words invoke a resounding "Amen" and other moments when you flinch because we've touched a raw and tender wound. For others of you who are new to the work and would like to glean from those of us who have walked the path ahead of you, this playbook was created so that you don't have to reinvent the wheel.

Wherever you find yourself on the spectrum of experience, we want you to know that you are not alone. No matter what it looks or feels like, please know that others have survived—and you will too. In fact, others have learned how to thrive in this work. Knowing that others have done it should encourage you. We serve a God who is a respecter of persons. If we can do it, so can you.

To those who would partner with the diversity professional (outlier, ally, or co-conspirator, which will be explained later), we want you to be a humble learner. We want you to hear, see, and deepen your commitment to diversity, inclusion, and equity within your organizations. We want you to acknowledge your privilege and *use it* to create a more inclusive community. We want you to celebrate with us. We want you to mourn with us. We want you to *listen*. We hope this book gives you the opportunity to do all the above.

To the organization, we want you to understand where you are, be encouraged to move forward, and learn from the past. Learn from your mistakes and the mistakes of other Christian organizations. Many Christian organizations have been complicit in the perpetuation of oppressive systems since their founding. While I believe there is a desire to change, change has been painful and slow moving for decades. We hope to give some concrete tools, steps, and examples for ways to move your organization forward in your diversity efforts. Change won't be easy. Change will come at a cost. However, if you do the work, you will see the results.

What This Isn't

We've stated the purpose in various ways above. However, we find it helpful to be clear about why we are writing this playbook. Let's start with what this playbook *isn't*. This playbook is not designed to bash any Christian organization. The organizations where we've worked and served have been both blessings and training grounds to us. We've learned about ourselves, our society, and our God through these organizations. We've grown in leadership, maturity, confidence, humility, and patience through these organizations. We've learned what to do and what *not* to do through these organizations. We've developed lifelong friendships and sowed thousands upon thousands of seeds at these organizations. Neither of us would trade our time at these places. They have shaped us into the people we are today.

This playbook is also not intended to be a comprehensive guide for diversity matters within Christian organizations. There is no way we could cover everything in one playbook. There is also no way you can learn everything you need to thrive in this work from the pages of a book. This work is about people. People thrive within community. There are some things that *must* be experienced. Your context matters. Your experiences and worldview matters. What you bring combined with the culture of your respective organization create a unique blend of circumstances. No one playbook can teach you how to survive and thrive in that environment. No one book can teach you how to be a good ally. No one book can help your organization become the inclusive beacon of light that is needed in today's world.

What This Is

However, here's what we *do* hope to accomplish with this playbook:

- For the diversity professionals:
  - We hope to assure you that you are not crazy. Yes, these things happen within Christian organizations. Yes, we experience disappointment and hurt. Yes, you can move past this and use these experiences to inform and educate.
  - We hope to provide you with basic survival tools that will help you navigate the turbulent waters that lie ahead.
  - We hope to encourage you that you are not alone, that others have gone before you, that people are here for you if you need help.
  - Most importantly, we hope you get to the last page of this book and *know* that the God of the universe has called you to this good work. As messy and painful as it is, the knowledge that God is with you and will be celebrating with you in the good times will sustain you through the hard times.
- For the outliers, allies, and co-conspirators:
  - We hope you feel the love and appreciation we have for the ways you've shown up over the years.
  - We hope you learn more about the struggle of diversity professionals and develop a greater sense of empathy and compassion.
  - We hope you are moved and galvanized by the stories.
  - We hope you are equipped to continue "fighting the good fight of faith" for the sake of the kingdom.
  - We hope to turn every outlier into an ally or a co-conspirator.
  - For the organizations:
  - We hope to give senior leadership some "insider" information that will assist with changing organizational culture and embracing diversity as a kingdom principle.
  - We hope to equip senior leaders and administrators with resources and best-practice tools.

- We hope to provoke senior leaders, administrators, and boards to make diversity and inclusion a priority that can be seen from the top down and within budgetary allocation.
- We hope senior leaders, administrators, and boards make *real* and *sustainable* change that leads to healthier organizational climates that are not toxic to marginalized communities (and thereby increase the retention of marginalized communities within the organization).

Format and Scope

Over the next fourteen chapters, we will talk about diversity from different vantage points within Christian organizations. In our experiences, one of the main reasons diversity efforts fail is that not everyone is reading the same playbook (we talk in depth about this issue in Chapter Eleven). Therefore, we've chosen to address three distinct audiences: the diversity professional; the outlier, ally, and co-conspirator; and the organization. Each audience has a distinct part to play in the success of diversity efforts within your organization. We encourage you to begin with the part that fits your role in the organization and then read the other parts. If everyone has the same playbook, then there is common language and greater accountability.

- In Part 1, our goal is personal. We want to encourage, uplift, and help develop the diversity professional within Christian organizations. We've included stories, examples, best practices, and practical tools to help navigate the rocky terrain of Christian organizations.
- In Part 2, our goal is pastoral. We define the distinction between the three groups and how they interact with the diversity professionals and with the organization as a whole. We want this group to understand that their voices matter and that they can be powerful forces for change within their organizations.
- In Part 3, our goal is prophetic. We speak directly to senior leadership, administrators, and board members—the ones who have the authority to disrupt systems and dismantle corrupt

structures—ending with the provocative question, "What does diversity success look like within your organization?"

We have tried to keep the book as relatable as possible. To that end, we've included stories, personal observations, and experiences. As with any coauthored project, we want to be as unified as possible while maintaining our distinctive voices. The fact that we have the same first name could also be confusing. To avoid that, when we are speaking as ourselves and sharing our individual experiences, we will indicate who is speaking by adding our names in parentheses at the beginning of the section (such as "Michelle L." or "Michelle W.").

A Word about How We Use the Term *Diversity*

As you read this playbook, you will notice that we use the term *diversity* in two ways. First, we use it in its truest definition: "the presence of difference." *Difference* could mean any or all social identities associated with being human: race, gender, social class, ability, sexual orientation, and others. (We are not addressing biological diversity in this book.) Second, we use the term *diversity* as shorthand for "diversity, inclusion, equity, reconciliation." In this way, we are using the term in the manner that is consistent with the average person. In Chapter Ten, "Shared Commitment," we explain the differences in the meanings of *diversity*, *inclusion*, *equity*, and *reconciliation*. When we want to specifically address inclusion, equity, or reconciliation, we will use those specific terms.

A Unique Moment in History

The last few years have been like no others in the history of our country. The level of hate speech, plus the blatant disrespect of women, people of color, immigrants, and anything that is *different* or *other* has become increasingly troublesome and deadly. Police brutality, Black Lives Matter, anti-Asian sentiments, the me-too movement, the church-too movement, transphobia, race riots—the list goes on and on. Rather than point fingers of blame and pontificate over causes and effects, we would like to invite you to consider this moment in history as an opportunity. This unique moment gives the diversity professional an opportunity to *shine*. It gives allies and co-conspirators a worldwide platform via social media to speak in solidarity. It gives outliers an opportunity to learn and choose how they will respond. It gives leaders of Christian organizations an opportunity to critically examine the practices and policies of their organizations. It gives Christian organizations an opportunity to lead with love.

We firmly believe that as Christians, we are all called upon to speak with grace and truth in this moment. We are called upon to help shape the discourse of this moment. We are called upon to allow space for young and old minds alike to process during this moment. We are called upon to prophetically lead during this moment. We, the authors, hope all who read this book know how strategically positioned they are to plant seeds, to water seeds, and to allow God to get the increase in this moment. For such a time as this, dear readers—for such a unique time as this.

Takeaways

We will end every chapter with a summary of key concepts. For this introduction, we would like to reiterate that diversity matters to God. We have all been called to walk this journey—the diversity professional, those seeking to partner with diversity professionals, and Christian organizations. You do not walk it alone. You *cannot* walk it alone. God is with you in this good work. Trust that it is *good* work! This good work is God's work.

PART ONE

FOR THE DIVERSITY PROFESSIONAL

CHAPTER 1

A SENSE OF CALLING

> *You did not choose me, but I chose you and appointed you so that you might go and bear fruit—fruit that will last—and so that whatever you ask in my name the Father will give you.*
> —John 15:16

The Bible is filled with stories of people feeling *called* by God to do a particular work, such as Paul proclaiming the gospel to the Gentiles and the disciples to be fishers of people. A *calling* is a "knowing" that God is inviting us to a particular work, a work that is aligned with our experiences, capabilities, and willingness to say yes to God's invitation. However, it is more than just using one's abilities to complete a particular task. No, a calling or sense of calling has a much deeper meaning—at least it has for the both of us.

For us, a sense of calling is the *motivation* for doing this work. *Calling*, not just skills and experience, is what led us to apply for the positions we have occupied and it is the reason we have stayed in our professions as long as we have. *Calling* is about saying, "Yes, I'll go," because we know that we have been saved by grace and positioned in our organizations for such a time as this. Below, we share our own stories of calling to this work in order to demonstrate that there are multiple paths to this work and to emphasize the importance of our faith to our work as diversity professionals.

The Power of Story: Thrown into the Fire (Michelle W.)

My first year as multicultural director was fraught with a series of unfortunate events. It was 2008 and the election of Barack Obama was a jubilant time for me and many of my loved ones. However, on college campuses the atmosphere was tense. On my Christian college campus in the heartland of America, tensions boiled over in the aftermath of the election. Social media reported the "n" word being used in conjunction with the new President of the United States. Nooses were hung from trees. Confrontations took place in classrooms. It was a trial by fire for this new employee, who was five months into the job.

This would have been enough to make anybody second guess their career choice. However, that wasn't the end. That academic year, an African American student reported a rape that ended up being a false report, and a student alleged severe discrimination in a prominent department. By the time commencement came around, I wanted to crawl into a hole and hide. Gratefully, these catalytic events highlighted the need for outside intervention. We hired an amazing diversity consultant (shout-out to Dr. Brenda) and began the process of assessing our climate.

While this first year was by far the worst, something happened every year that caused me to question my sanity and vocational calling. I wish there had been a resource like this when I was struggling to make sense of the unique world that is Christian higher education. To be clear, all of us go into this work with rose-colored, faith-enhanced glasses. We believe the *Christian* in front of *higher education* means something. We believe it means our organizations and the people who work and take classes there hold a set of values consistent with the life and message of Jesus Christ.

Therefore, when the actions of our organizations and the people who work and study there do *not* reflect the love ethic of Christ, we are disappointed (to say the least). It is probably more accurate to say that we are disillusioned, disheartened, and completely distressed. This was my experience. How could people who claim to love Jesus disregard the humanity of their fellow human beings?

My Family Story

As with so many of us, I was hired into this position with no previous experience in cross-cultural communications, ethnic studies, or inter-cultural education. I had been a social worker for fifteen years and was an ordained minister. Despite my lack of formal education in the subject matter, my life experiences played a major role in my development as a diversity professional.

As I was growing up, my father was a retail manager and then became a district manager. His career demanded that our family move every two years or so. We always moved to an area that was primarily White. By the time I was sixteen, I had moved nine times within suburbia Midwest (Ohio, Indiana, and Michigan). Needless to say, I became adept at living bicul-turally. My mother made sure we maintained close ties with the African American community (via church) wherever we moved. This personal experience prepared me for a lifelong journey as a "bridge" person.

I remember being one of five African Americans in my entire middle school. I had to purchase hair care products downtown on Sundays when we went to church because none of the stores in our own community car-ried them. I remember being teased for talking "White" by my cousins when we visited them. I remember being told I was "cute for a Black girl" by my blue-eyed, blond-haired neighbor, whom I secretly had a crush on. I remember knowing that I couldn't go into certain neighbors' yards because I saw the way they looked at my siblings and me. These are things I learned at an early age. The lesson that I was "different" or "other" was repeated almost daily while I was growing up.

When I was sixteen, my parents divorced and my siblings and I moved to a more diverse community. This was a cultural adjustment for me. I went from being the "cool Black girl" to just one of the crowd. There are things you become accustomed to when you are in the minority. You learn how to laugh off the jokes, you learn how to walk away just to keep the peace, and most important, you learn how to survive. Most of the time, survival equates to assimilation. I didn't realize how much of my identity had been suppressed until my last two years of high school.

College Years

College is its own cultural environment. Everyone experiences culture shock. Identity is tested and developed during undergraduate school in ways that define who you will be thereafter. This was certainly the case with me. I was accepted to the University of Cincinnati, and I was giddy as my mom and aunt helped me finish decorating my side of the suite on move-in day. I was the first to arrive. I had communicated with my roommate by phone and letter (it was before the days of the Internet). After we finished decorating, we left to get something to eat and roam the campus.

A couple of hours later, I said goodbye and went back up to my room. Lo and behold, my other suitemates had arrived. We had a quad—there were four of us. As I walked into the room, I immediately stopped in my tracks. Hanging on the wall at the entrance to the suite was a HUGE Confederate flag. I was frozen in place and fear gripped me as I had never known before. I vaguely heard someone trying to get my attention. My suitemate shook me and asked, "Are you all right?" I nodded and focused on the person trying to get my attention.

I had exchanged correspondence with all my quadmates, so I knew a little about each of them. As I listened to the girl in front of me talk, I realized she was the one who had hung the flag. I made some excuse and walked out of the room. So many things were going through my mind at that time. I wished I hadn't let my mother leave. I wondered if there was any way to change rooms. I couldn't believe she could just talk to me and have no idea why I would be so upset about THAT flag. I marched over to the Resident Director's apartment and asked her to follow me. We went back into the room, and I pointed at the flag. The flag girl stared at me and was perplexed. What followed was one of the best mediated conversations I've ever had. To this day, I think back on the skill with which that RD listened and asked questions of both of us.

It turns out, the flag girl was ignorant of what that flag represented to me. To her, it was a symbol of pride. As with hanging an American flag, it represented her heritage. It was a piece of her identity. To me, it represented the institution of slavery, a cruel and oppressive system that treated my ancestors like cattle and ripped apart families. After our conversation, the flag girl agreed to take the flag down. She was actually appalled that the flag had produced that type of response in someone. I was pretty flabbergasted by her lack of awareness. However, the only way either of us discovered this was through dialogue.

There were other instances in undergrad that highlighted the stark realities of prejudice, bias, and ignorance. There were also instances in which I became aware of my own knowledge gaps concerning African American history and culture. I was confronted with my personal biases and prejudices as well. These lessons continued well beyond my college years.

Postgraduate Life

When I was hired as the multicultural director at the Christian college I referred to earlier, I had no formal education in cross-cultural or ethnic studies. I had been a social worker for fifteen years and was an ordained minister. Neither my degree in psychology nor my life experiences prepared me for the trial by fire that was my first year in this position.

The traumatic events that occurred during this first year became the catalyst for change on our campus, and I spent the next seven years helping to create a more inclusive campus community. I was promoted to the position of director of the Cultural Resource Center and eventually as assistant dean of students.

When I felt God calling me to pursue something different, I knew I wanted to marry my passion for student development with my love for the church. So I transitioned to the role of dean of students at a graduate seminary on the East Coast. In this capacity, I was able to continue my role as a bridge builder through my embodied presence at senior leadership tables. I was able to directly impact the future of the church by training and equipping future ministers. In December 2018, I resigned from my three-and-a-half-year assignment at the seminary with the intention of continuing our relationship in a consultant capacity if needed.

A Matter of Life and Death

"I can put you on medication, you can change your eating habits and adopt an exercise regiment, but ultimately it will be stress that kills you." My doctor said these sobering words to me in the spring of 2018 as she mentioned health issues that have plagued my family for generations. I was going down the same path—but at an accelerated rate because of stress. Stressful job + inability to say no + a conditioned "martyr" personality + circumstances that contributed to flimsy boundaries = change of lifestyle.

I have to be honest with you: this was a hard decision. It is counter-cultural and counterintuitive. Everything in me revolted at the idea of slowing down. However, it was a matter of life and death. So I decided to take a year off, a sabbatical of sorts. It was an amazing time of self-discovery, traveling, and reconnection with God. As I reflect on this season of rest and reflection, I am keenly aware of the self-inflicted and society-approved pressure to perform at all costs. My hope is that in this next chapter of my life, I can model and assist others to prioritize self-care. I am particularly interested in those who work in service industries (teachers, clergy, non-profit leaders, social workers, counselors, crisis responders, and so on). All of us know that those who engage in the work of diversity and reconciliation fall into that category. I've had too many friends whose quality of life and health have been adversely impacted doing this work. That is why I've chosen to write this diversity playbook.

Who, Me? No Way! (Michelle L.)

I was an undergraduate student more than forty years ago. If on the day I graduated from my undergraduate college someone had told me that within forty years I would become a college professor and an executive-level administrator for the college I had just graduated from, I would not have believed them. Who, me? No way! I had other plans—plans that would take me far from the Midwest, plans far from the academy, plans far from Christian higher education. Well, as the saying goes, "You want to make God laugh—tell him your plans." I shared my heart's desires about vocation with God in prayer. Instead of confirmation of what I wanted, I kept being guided down a path I never imagined, a path I had never even conceived as being a possibility for me.

My Early Years

I was born in San Diego, California, to loving newlyweds on a military base in the early hours of a winter morning. I was their first child. My father was in the Navy, and we were a military family until 1975, when I entered high school. My father served twenty years in the Navy, and his location of service changed every three to four years. This meant that my family moved often. From what my parents have told me, much of the time, my father would be home every day in time for dinner, but there were a few times when he was stationed on a ship for several months, and my mother, brothers, and I would stay behind. I do not recall those times when my father was absent.

I was born in San Diego, but the time I spent there was very short. At the age of six months, we moved to Georgia. From Georgia we moved to Germany—where my oldest brother was born. We are two years apart in age. From Germany we moved back stateside to Virginia—where my youngest brother was born. We are five years apart in age. From Virginia we moved to Illinois, from Illinois to Alaska, from Alaska to Puerto Rico, from Puerto Rico to Michigan, where my sister was born. We are fifteen years apart in age.

My family lived a short while with my great-grandmother (my father's grandmother) while my parents looked for a more permanent place to live. I spent half of seventh grade attending a middle school within walking distance from my great-grandmother's house. I still remember walking home for lunch every day. I enjoyed staying with my great-grandmother because we were able to live in an all-Black neighborhood. More often than not as I was growing up, my family and I lived in predominantly White neighborhoods, and I attended nearly all-White schools. My parents frequently informed me that being Black meant having to be twice as good to achieve half as much. And if we wanted to overcome the racism that was designed to keep us down, we had to work hard and behave in ways that were always above any appearance of misconduct.

There was never a question of *if* I was going to attend college. The only question was *where*. My parents were firm believers in education as the path for a better life—especially for Black folks. As a student at a midsized Christian liberal arts college, I didn't realize how much of an anomaly I was. During my years as an undergraduate student, only 0.2 percent of the student body were non-White and less than 10 percent were not affiliated with the denomination that owned the college. I was Black. I saw myself as non-denominational, and I didn't intend on changing my religious affiliation—I just wanted a good education and to be close to home. I graduated with a degree in sociology and had planned to use that degree for a career in retail sales; but encouraged by my parents, I went to graduate school. "If you aren't tired, keep going," they said. "We'll find a way to pay for it some way. Just keep going." I did keep going and graduated from a large secular university with master's and doctorate degrees in sociology.

From Faculty to Executive Leadership

My career as a faculty member in Christian higher education started in January 1985 at the college I had attended as an undergraduate. I was hired to teach a three-week class based on my dissertation research on achievement and self-esteem among African American adults. I was almost finished with my graduate work; all I had to do was complete my dissertation. My plans were to pick up a paycheck for the three weeks, grind out completing my dissertation, and then start applying for jobs in larger urban areas.

Three weeks turned into a year as an adjunct instructor, which then turned into a tenure-track position in the department of sociology. I eventually earned tenure and become the department chair. Life was good. Not perfect or without disappointments concerning the progress on issues of diversity by the college, but all in all, I enjoyed teaching and had the perfect teaching schedule. I never wanted to be a diversity professional. I taught a lot about diversity; but teaching the next generation about sociology was enough for me.

I had been teaching for about twenty years when I was approached to become the second dean for multicultural affairs. This position was housed in the academic division and reported to the provost. My initial response was no. There was a failed search, and I was asked again to consider the position. I prayed about it and felt a nudging by the Holy Spirit to accept and agreed to fill the vacancy—but only for a year as an interim until a permanent person could be found. However, I served the college in that capacity for nine years. A new search committee for the dean of multicultural affairs, a position I was filling on an interim basis, was never assembled. Hmmm, I wonder how that happened. I discovered that I enjoyed administrative work. Having found a deeper sense of accomplishment and purpose in the work, I was content with being a dean and thought I would stay in that position until I retired—but God had other plans for me.

In 2013 the college hired a new president. One of his priorities was to expand his cabinet to include the college chaplain and a point person for diversity. In 2015 a national search was conducted. I applied for the position and was hired as the inaugural chief diversity officer. It is a position that I still hold as of this writing. The chief diversity officer is a cabinet-level position reporting to the president. The primary responsibility of this role is leading deep, meaningful, and pervasive changes in the way the campus understands and practices diversity and inclusion. I have been working in Christian higher education for over thirty-five years and as the CDO for over eight years. It is humbling to be able to see some of the seeds I have planted over the years bear fruit and gratifying to have the support of my president and to be able to work with colleagues across the campus on diversity issues. My career in Christian higher education has been a long one, but it almost didn't happen. There were several times when I questioned my calling to a predominately White Christian campus in particular and to diversity work in general. Perhaps the greatest time of questioning came when I visited the slave castles of Ghana and South Africa.

Slave Castles

In the summer of 2007 I visited South Africa, and in the autumn of the same year I returned to the African continent to visit Ghana. On both occasions I was in Africa as an extension of my work as a dean. The two visits were three months apart; but on each trip, I visited buildings that once held slaves. In South Africa I visited the Slave Lodge Museum in Cape Town, and in Ghana I visited the Elmina Slave Castle. Both experiences touched me in the same way as I came face-to-face with the reality that Christians were involved in the trafficking of African people. Both times I heard tour guides tell of the involvement of the White ethnic group that founded my school and the complicity of a branch of the denomination that owned my school. Both times I questioned if I could return to my job at my college.

I had a sickening feeling in my stomach when I visited the Slave Lodge and the Elmina Slave Castle by the thought of so many of my African ancestors being held in inhumane conditions, of so many being transported to the Americas, and that Christian men—some with the same last names as the people I now worked with—could sing praises to God in a chapel built above the cells where African women were kept in bondage. I was sickened by the thought of religion being used to justify and not liberate the captivity of African people.

This same theology that was used to justify the captivity of African people formed the theological foundations of the school where I worked. I decided not to leave my place of employment because I felt God had me there for a particular assignment. I could not leave because I believed it was what God was requiring of me in spite of the hurt I felt. I believed that if God were asking me to do something that appeared difficult, God must have a plan that I didn't know the fullness of. Believe me, I wrestled with God about staying—I even have a limp to show for it. There were many nights that I cried, many days that I fasted and prayed, and times—if I am honest—that I told God it was too much to ask and I was done. But I have always sought to live my life in alignment with what I believe is God's purpose and plan for my life. I had to lean in—I mean really, really lean in—to trusting God despite what I felt.

Bearing Witness

When I started on this path of higher education, nobody said it would be easy. But I didn't expect it to be as hard as it was. I wish I knew then what I know now. It is impossible to go back in time and it is impossible to make up for lost time. I have so much lost time in my life. Time I cannot account for during my childhood and time I lost as a scholar because I was not connected to people who looked like me. My life in academia has felt like the lyrics of the James Weldon Johnson song "Lift Every Voice and Sing." The lyrics speak of personal and collective weariness and tears of the descendants of those brought to the United States as slaves—my people. The lyrics, however, are not just about victimhood. They speak of God's faithfulness in hard places, God's protection, and pride in an African heritage.

Finding protection in God's loving hand, I have come a long way. By God's grace I have been able to work within Christian organizations as a teacher and leader and work with Christian organizations as a consultant to bring about awareness and better practices of diversity. God's faithfulness to me and God's love for marginalized people has deepened my commitment and passion for this area of kingdom work. I believe I have learned a few things along the way, and I am still learning something new every day.

I am writing this book because I want to bear witness to the fact that it is possible for people of color to flourish in Christian higher education and within predominately White Christian organizations. I want to encourage the next generation of diversity professionals in Christian organizations and to share the lessons I have learned on my journey as a diversity professional in hopes that their journey will be smoother than mine.

....

Why do we do this? It is certainly not for the money. It is not one of those vocations you can survive in if you just stumble upon it, filling a position, but have no heart for the work. We do it because we feel called to this work. It's a calling similar to the assignment of Jesus, which he knew would lead him to the cross. He knew that *he had to go* through the *messy, painful* agony that was the cross for humankind to be reconciled to God. This calling demands that we die to ourselves and to our preconceived notions and biases. This calling demands that we face the messy, painful reality of sin in the form of -isms, divisions, and schisms.

We do this because we believe God has uniquely prepared us from the foundation of the world to serve in this capacity. Our journeys have led us to this vocational path. We do this because we believe God loves the entirety of the diverse creation and longs for us to live out the "love mandate" (Matt. 22:36–40). We do this out of obedience. We do this out of love.

All in a Day's Work

If there were a playlist that accompanied our journeys as diversity professionals, one of the songs that would have to be included is gospel artist James Cleveland's 1978 "I Don't Feel No Ways Tired." If you are not familiar with the song, it speaks of feeling energized though experiencing hardships because of God's faithfulness. The lyrics are repetitive, simulating a rocking within one's soul. If you have never seen Cleveland sing the song either in person or heard a recording, you should look up a YouTube video of him singing the song, because just reading the lyrics doesn't do the song justice.

Our journeys, individually and collectively, have been filled with highs, lows, and everything in between. We have succeeded against the odds, flourished in desert places, felt supported in our organizations, felt isolated in our organizations, and experienced the emotions of joy, anger, fear, disappointment, rage, surprise, and empowerment. The range of emotions is typical, and if you consider the nature of the work, it should be no surprise. You could even experience all these emotions in a single day. I know there have been several times when that's been true for me (Michelle L.). For example, one day I received word from an organization that had been commissioned to conduct an antiracism audit that my organization had reached the highest level of certification. Oh, the *joy*! It had taken three years of hard work—programing and policy development—to achieve this milestone, and at the time, we were the only higher education institution to reach this level. I had led the work. I felt affirmed, seen, and valued. I was proud of my institution. (Hmm—was this the time to ask for a raise?)

But all the good vibes were overshadowed within two hours of receiving the news when at the regular meeting of my diversity council I shared the good news and asked for volunteers to accompany me to the award ceremony in a month. The response from half the council (not an exaggeration) was *not* to publicize the fact that we had received the award—*not* announce it in any of the institution's media outlets, and *not* publish it on our internal newsletter. What? In that moment, I felt disappointed, angry, and alone. Those who did not want to publish the good news felt that by publishing it, the institution would be implying that we had "arrived" and there was no more work to be done. This was not the message that I or the auditing organization promoted. The certification was acknowledgment that we were on the right path and were submitting ourselves for outside accountability.

So what happened? I announced the award and attended the award ceremony anyway. I invited those who were supportive from the council and other key campus stakeholders to attend the award ceremony. We had a great time celebrating, all the while acknowledging that there was more work to be done. As diversity professionals working to advance diversity, inclusion, and equity initiatives, we find that the range of emotions is part and parcel with the nature of this work. Nobody told us the road would be easy, but we do it anyway. It's all in a day's work.

As a diversity professional, you will have times when you feel hidden away and think your work is going unnoticed (especially when you're changing infrastructures and everything seems peaceful). You'll also have times when you're in the spotlight and your work is celebrated. You'll have weary days when it feels as if the world rests on your shoulders—and your shoulders alone. There will be seasons when there is too much to do and not enough time to do it. There will also be (or should be—you may have to fight for them) seasons when you experience a Zen-like flow of work. There will be times when you will receive full credit for your work, no credit for your work, and shared credit for *your* work. We know because we have experienced it all, and every other diversity professional we have spoken with has had the same experience. It's all in a day's work.

Yes, leading diversity efforts is hard work. It is complex. It is frustrating. It is exhilarating. Such is the nature of the work. And it is also the nature of the calling from God to do this work within Christian organizations. One would think that because diversity, inclusion, equity, and reconciliation are part of what it means to live kingdom-minded—to live as followers of Christ—this work would be easy to accomplish within Christian organizations.

Such is not the case. As with all of creation, the church, Christian organizations, and Christ followers have all been affected by the fall. The fall has broken our relationship with God and one another. The fall has broken the systems and institutions intended to improve life in community. The fall has cleared the way for -isms to become established in our hearts and our organizations. That's why this work is no easier within Christian organizations. Thanks be to God for Jesus. Because of Jesus we know that *better* is possible. Because of Jesus we are not without hope, "For he himself is our peace, who has made the two groups one and has destroyed the barrier, the dividing wall of hostility" (Eph. 2:14).

Takeaways

When you know you are called, even when times get tough, you have an assurance. When you are called to kingdom work, you know you have heavenly backup. Even better, you are covered on *all* sides! This doesn't mean that difficult times don't touch you. It does mean that when difficult times come, the God of the universe is with you. Don't be discouraged because your calling narrative doesn't look or sound like someone else's. We all have different journeys. Even in this, we see God's celebration of diversity. When you are called to be a diversity professional, you must accept and embrace this truth: "We may never see the end results, but that is the difference between the master builder and the worker. We are workers, not master builders; ministers, not messiahs. We are prophets of a future not our own."[1]

---

[1] This prayer was first presented by Cardinal John Dearden in 1979 and quoted by Pope Francis in 2015. This reflection is an excerpt from a homily written for Cardinal Dearden by then-Fr. Ken Untener on the occasion of the Mass for Deceased Priests, October 25, 1979. Pope Francis quoted Cardinal Dearden in his remarks to the Roman Curia on December 21, 2015. Fr. Untener was named bishop of Saginaw, Michigan, in 1980.

CHAPTER 2

THE NEED FOR ALLIES AND CO-CONSPIRATORS

*When Moses' hands grew tired, they took a stone and put
it under him and he sat on it. Aaron and Hur held his
hands up—one on one side, one on the other—so that his
hands remained steady till sunset.*

—Exodus 17:12

The work of diversity professionals on Christian campuses and within
Christian organizations can be lonely and frustrating. Okay, to be
honest, that's anywhere—not just Christian organizations. We know
because we have worked in both Christian and secular contexts, but
our work as diversity professionals has been situated primarily within
Christian contexts. We have each worked in environments where there
were *no* diversity professionals and those places can be even lonelier for
those seeking to advance diversity and inclusion initiatives within their
organizations. So why is this work so lonely and frustrating at times?

Every organization is different, every diversity professional is different, and what diversity professionals need in order to personally flourish
and to institute changes in their organization is different. But one thing
remains true: diversity professionals—whether the solo professional

or a division with several diversity professionals—cannot do this work alone. Diversity professionals need allies and co-conspirators. (Note: A deeper discussion on allies and co-conspirators is covered in Chapter Seven. For now, suffice it to say that allies and co-conspirators are people who do not work in the diversity field who partner with diversity professionals to advance diversity, inclusion, and equity within their organizations.)

We need individuals who want to partner with diversity professionals: partners—allies and co-conspirators—who see and understand the intentional and unintentional structural, cultural, and interpersonal barriers that breed and sustain unwelcoming environments. We need people who understand that diversity is broad in scope, intersectionality is real, and that in order to achieve real change, the interlocking systems of racism, sexism, classism, heterosexism, ableism, and so on must be addressed. A helpful ally and co-conspirator not only sees and understands the various dimensions of diversity but also shares the sense of urgency for things to change. And perhaps most significantly, allies and co-conspirators desire to be engaged in the process of bringing about change and/or supporting those who are working to bring about change.

Diversity professionals need individuals who "have their backs"— individuals who are familiar with the culture of an organization and can alert diversity professionals when they are headed into an institutional "buzz saw" or about to step on a political landmine or about to knock over a sacred cow. Good allies and co-conspirators do not intentionally work to undermine initiatives that diversity professionals are trying to implement. Allies and co-conspirators are "safe" people—individuals who provide safe spaces and sturdy shoulders for venting frustrations, sharing worries and concerns, and allowing a diversity professional to be vulnerable with their feelings and innermost thoughts. Good allies and co-conspirators are good listeners and creative thinkers and provide feedback on ideas. Diversity professionals *need* allies and co-conspirators.

Diversity professionals need people to share the emotional, psychological, and vocational loads they carry in this work. Just as Moses needed Aaron and Hur to hold up his hands in the midst of a battle, diversity professionals need people to stand with them when the work gets too heavy.

To be clear, we are not talking about allies and co-conspirators to speak for or do the work of diversity professionals. Diversity professionals are (or should be) hired because they possess the skill sets and experience that match a perceived institutional need. However, when new to an institution or new to an administrative role, diversity professionals may lack knowledge about how an institution gets things done. To be clear, within a new role or new institution, diversity professionals do not lack ideas about what needs to be done, but they may lack knowledge of the hidden rules and of who the movers and shakers are within an organization. When taking on the role, diversity professionals are aware of the expectations and outcomes outlined in their job descriptions (assuming there is a job description in place). However, they may not be aware of the hidden agendas and assumptions that were in place when the job descriptions were constructed. Diversity professionals need allies and co-conspirators who will work with them as they strive to activate change and transformation within an organization. Allies and co-conspirators are not optional. Let's repeat this for the people in the back of the room: allies and co-conspirators are not optional.

Help with Understanding Historical Contexts

Like people, institutions have complex histories, and as we mentioned above, it is important to have an ally and co-conspirator in your corner who knows the history of your organization and how that history has impacted diversity and inclusion initiatives within the organization. The regional/geographical location, church affiliation, founders, donors, board of trustees, and constituencies all directly or indirectly influence the culture of an organization. How these factors influence an organization would ideally be known *before* the incoming diversity professional accepts their new role. The ideal is not always possible, and sometimes understanding all these influences is something not taught but rather caught. Sometimes these influences have to be experienced to be fully understood.

Questions that can be asked to help one understand how these influences impact diversity efforts include, but are not limited to, the following: In what part of the country (or in what country) is the organization located? What is the compositional diversity within the area? What is the compositional diversity of the organization? Is this a new position, or a position that has been in place but is being restructured? If this is a new or restructured position, is it because of an incident; and if so, was the incident public and how widely known is it (as in, did it become a national news story)? (In 2020 and 2021, we witnessed a number of Christian and secular organizations quickly create Vice President of Diversity positions. We know because we were both inundated with requests to either apply or recommend people that we knew. So yes, it's a thing.) Does the organization have community partners? What is the composition of those partnering organizations? When was the organization founded and by whom? Was the organization founded on a premise of inclusion or exclusion? Is there a denominational affiliation? How diverse is the denomination? When was the last climate survey conducted and what were the results? What have the diversity challenges been? Who named them as challenges? What was the last complaint about diversity? Who brought it and how was it handled? (Remember that diversity is not about simply race, but also gender, sexual orientation, social class, abilities, and so on.) Who was tasked with seeking a remedy? Who was not consulted but should have been (you will know this by follow-up complaints)? And what statements of commitment to diversity, inclusion, and equity have come from an organization's governing body (board, executive team, extended administrative team, senior staff), and when were they issued?

Most organizations have documents that can answer these questions. Finding people who know where the documents are can sometimes lead you to allies and co-conspirators. Documentation of how an organization has been thinking (or not thinking) about diversity can often be found in meeting notes, organizational identity documents, newspaper archives, or the files of the local historian. Community organizations dedicated to advancing the cause of diversity, inclusion, and equity may also be a source of information. The historical roots of an organization play a major role in the current and lived realities of our diverse communities. It behooves us as diversity professionals to do our research and discover the intentions of the founders of our organizations along with those who will be able to give us a thorough timeline of the diversity efforts that have taken place before our arrival. It also behooves us as diversity professionals to get to know the keepers of community and organizational histories.

However, it is also important to note that some individuals who are the keepers of community or organizational histories may not be allies and co-conspirators. Some will be, but others may not be, and that's okay—they are still sources of valuable information. When I (Michelle W.) was hired at my last job, I immediately launched a "weeding-out" process that I called a "listening tour." I set up short meetings over coffee or lunch to get to know individuals. One of my main objectives was to try establishing where people landed on the "diversity" spectrum. I (Michelle L.) have often found that organizational archivists are so happy that anyone has asked them to search for historical information that they locate the information quickly and provide even more than what was requested. Most archivists I have known would not identify themselves as allies nor would they identify themselves as disruptive outliers. Rather, they identify as people who are just doing their job and the work they love.

We have also found the same to be true for some human resource professionals we have worked with when disaggregated hiring and retention data by race, gender, or some other social category was needed. They were happy to provide historical information when clarity about the reason for the requested information was provided. It also helped to provide a deadline for when the information was needed and to inquire about their ability to meet the deadline.

In consulting, we have both benefited from information that long-time employees have been willing to share with us as we sought to understand the unwritten history of an organization more fully. They weren't necessarily on the diversity bus, so to speak, but were willing to share their observations and experiences. And from their experiences we better understand what has failed in the past, the tensions of the present, and the hopes for the future.

We believe everyone lands somewhere on the spectrum from completely disinterested to wholeheartedly passionate. More on this when we have the "where to find allies" conversation and in part two, which covers "Outliers, Allies, and Co-conspirators." What is important at this time is to note that I (Michelle W.) learned to do this because of a prior experience. When I was first hired on at a Christian college, my supervisor organized a "meet and greet" with the faculty and staff of color. This was a small but committed group. The six of us met for lunch that first time and vowed to continue the tradition. My supervisor initiated this because of the history of the position I had stepped into. Unbeknownst to me, the role had been in constant flux for the previous ten years. People came and went, the issues remained, and the role desperately needed stability.

These are things I learned from that group of faculty and staff of color. They shared some of their hurts, pains, and disappointments with the institution and also their hopes. These people were in their positions because they enjoyed their jobs and had a fondness for the institution. They were able to share messy truths while still expressing their support for the good work I was about to embark on. Over the years, I learned so much from that group. They were able to point me in the direction of several departments and people who historically supported diversity efforts.

Who's Your Ally?

Allies and co-conspirators are an important part of the work. However, a few words of caution are in order. Be wary of people who identify themselves as allies and co-conspirators before you have even had a chance to get to know them. They may, in fact, be allies and co-conspirators—but people do not get to identify themselves as such. The person the individual is trying to ally themselves with is the one who makes that call. You as the diversity professional decide who is and who is not your ally. One way of telling who has your back is by the advice they give you. Generally, when it is unsolicited advice, it's someone else's agenda. However, occasionally that impromptu meeting in the hallway where someone offers you advice you didn't ask for is divinely orchestrated. As diversity professionals, we need to be discerning about the intent of the person who is speaking in our ear.

I (Michelle L.) offer this story to you as an example of this very point. Over the years, I have had few well-meaning, self-proclaimed allies help without first asking if their help was something I needed or if what they were planning was something that would be helpful. One such situation came about midway through my career when I was still the dean for multicultural affairs. A faculty member of color was up for tenure and it was rumored that this faculty member was not likely to be approved for it.

Some suspected the reasoning for this was based on race, and others speculated job performance.

A group of White students felt the need to do something. In their words, they wanted to support the faculty member of color and draw attention to the school's missed opportunity to promote diversity. These self-proclaimed allies, without consulting me, created a spoof version of our thirty-plus-page antiracism statement. The spoof version appeared on campus without identifying the authors or the students' intention. The contents were so offensive that many of our students of color were afraid to leave their dorm rooms; they felt unsafe and like the mysterious publication was a statement about them not belonging as students. Parents were calling. The fallout was unanticipated by these self-proclaimed student "allies."

A town hall meeting was called. Sorrow was expressed, but the damage had been done. The self-proclaimed student allies had meant well, but they had not helped the faculty member up for tenure. They frightened students of color and made more work for me and the other diversity professionals on campus. Had they consulted me or other diversity professionals on campus, we could have let them know of more effective ways of protest—ways that would not cause harm for students of color. Just because I am in an executive-level position doesn't mean that I don't like a good (emphasis on good) protest every now and then. While I have not organized a protest, I have participated in several and even secured the support of campus security and other executive leaders. The moment that still brings a tear to my eyes when I think about it is when our director of campus safety walked with me to lead a student-initiated Black Lives Matter march on campus; and yes, he is White. The students alerted me to their plan and allowed me to provide guidance. The students felt affirmed and that they could trust our campus officers because they walked with them that day.)

Where to Look?

As the saying goes, "If you want a friend, *be* a friend." This maxim can be applied to finding an ally and co-conspirator. If you want a partner, be a partner. This means developing empathy toward someone else's challenges and issues. The challenges and issues do not have to be diversity related, but it wouldn't hurt if they were diversity related. For example, you could become an ally to someone who was in your new employee orientation group and whose work has a different diversity focus. For example, you are focused on race and they are focused on LGBTQ concerns; or you could strive to be a co-conspirator to someone who has been working in another department or division on sustainability matters. In becoming an ally or co-conspirator to someone else, you develop and deepen a relationship—a strategic relationship. Deepened relationships are fertile ground for finding your own allies and co-conspirators. When people feel that you care about the things that concern them, they are more likely to care for the things that concern *you*.

Other places within your organization to look for partners in your work include, but are not limited to, affinity group gatherings, administrators, trustees, directors of programing or projects, human resources officers, organizational archivists, long-time staff members, and members of the diversity committee. Some of these individuals carry job titles that may intuitively lead you to seeking them out as partners—for example, the director of multicultural student services, the chair of the diversity committee, or the vice president for workplace equality. However, sometimes the person you least expect to be a partner can become one, especially a partner for a specific issue—or example, the human resources director, a campus librarian, the director of community partnerships, or the vice president for advancement. It all depends upon what resources someone has at their disposal and their willingness to use those resources to help you or your project to flourish. It also depends upon the type of partner you are looking for. Whatever kind of partner—ally or co-conspirator—you are looking for, make the time to find one and allow time for a relationship to develop.

While it is natural to think that every member of a marginalized group is a potential partner, this has not always been the case for us. We have learned the hard way not to assume that every marginalized person will be an ally. For example, while people of color are often invested in matters of diversity, particularly around the topic of race, not everyone has the desire or luxury to be on a diversity committee or to help with launching a diversity initiative. In fact, one of the problems people of color run into when hired for a nondiversity-focused job is the pressure to serve on diversity committees or be the diversity spokesperson in times of crisis. Some call it the "color tax"—the tax of more being asked of you because your skin is black, brown, yellow, or red. And to be clear, generally speaking, the "more" that is being asked is good work but often doesn't count during performance reviews. It is *extra* work that takes time away from the work the person was actually hired to do. And let's not forget that some people who have marginalized identities just don't want to serve the organization in that way. There is wisdom in the verse "Know them which labour among you" (1 Thess. 5:12 KJV).

Knowing those who labor among you means moving past assumptions of people's interests based on skin color, gender, or longevity at an organization. Just as one should beware assuming that every person of color would be a good diversity ally, a person should also avoid the danger of assuming every White person is a White nationalist at worst or "just doesn't get it" at best. Move past assumptions and have conversations with people to really know their hearts. And more than knowing their hearts, know their willingness to act. Partners come in every skin color, ethnicity, nationality, gender, sexual orientation, and position within the organization. Partners are those who support diversity professionals, share their expertise and time, and leverage their social capital to advance diversity initiatives. And we can't stress enough the importance of cultivating a diverse set of partners. Allies and co-conspirators from a broad reach across the organization will aid you in the long term.

As was mentioned earlier, conducting a "listening tour" (a series of meetings with employees, students, clients, administrators, board members, and community partners) when you first arrive at an organization is a great way to discover where an individual's passions lie. After conducting the listening tour that I (Michelle W.) referred to above, I learned of specific countries that held significant meaning for professors. In turn, I was able to send students who needed funding assistance to travel abroad in those countries to the professors who had a heart for those areas of the world. This wasn't always successful, but often it yielded fruit. To be clear, the individuals whom I met on my listening tour varied in their interest in diversity, inclusion, and equity issues. However, it was a building block to forming more substantive relationships. Obviously, discernment was needed to discover who was an ally and who was not. The point here is that an intentional "getting to know you" strategy is needed to determine who your partners may be.

Moving on When Trust Is Broken

Unfortunately, sometimes the trust we have placed in an ally is broken. Someone may have taken credit for work that you have done. Someone may have said they would do one thing and then did another—something that left you "holding the bag" of responsibility. Someone may have acted in a way that indicates that they are not as far along in their own journey of cultural competence as you had first believed. Or someone misrepresented your words and efforts to others. Whatever the reason, a choice now must be made about whether the relationship can be saved or if it is time to move on.

Moving on is painful but at times necessary. Whether we choose to move on as continued partners or move on as colleagues, we *must* move on. Often these things work out for the better (imagine that). There have been several times when students have dropped subtle (and not-so-subtle) hints regarding the degree of "wokeness" of a faculty/staff colleague. Never underestimate the astuteness of your students if you are in an educational setting. They are sometimes more attuned than you because of relational bias. There have been times when a church parishioner has expressed concerns about a church staff member—concerns that confirmed the little "hmm" feeling you have experienced when working with the same staff member. It's always good to pay attention to how staff members interact with clients and others, not just how they interact with you. It doesn't always mean that a staff member is not a decent person or needs to be fired, but it may mean that the staffer is one way with you and another way with others.

Like everything in life, change should be expected. The department or person who has historically showed up for you may not always show up or stand up for diversity, inclusion, and equity issues within your organization. Expect that. Don't take it personally. Chalk it up to a shift in priorities or realignment. The great thing about this faith walk is that we trust God to put the right people in our path at the right times.

Takeaways

There are no "lone wolves" in this work. You cannot do this without partners—allies and co-conspirators. Be intentional about getting to know people within your organization. Don't be surprised when an unlikely individual becomes a partner. If you want partners, you have to be a partner. Pray and ask God for discernment regarding whom to establish relationships with. This process of discerning takes time. Remember that you are building mutually beneficial relationships. Rome wasn't built in a day and neither will your circle of allies and co-conspirators. Be patient and watch God honor your need for partners.

LONGEVITY IS POSSIBLE WITH SELF-CARE

Dear friend, I pray that you may enjoy good health and that all may go well with you, even as your soul is getting along well.
—3 John 2

Diversity professionals, new and seasoned, spend a lot of emotional and social capital planning, building, engaging, and responding— planning for new initiatives, building organizational capacity, engaging new ideas, and responding to crises big and small. Diversity profession- als spend a lot of their time taking care of their organizations and others. And at times it may seem like a thankless job. The pace of change is slower than we would want as we find ourselves explaining again why diversity is important; responding to yet another phone call from a complaining community member; and being invited to meetings only for the illusion of paying attention to diversity issues.

Pouring out our hearts day in and day out is draining. And if we are honest, some days we may wonder if it's all worth it. Many have said that it is *not* worth it and have left their organizations, some have left Christendom altogether. We have not. We, and many like us, have stayed. We have stuck it out. We have had long careers in diversity work and have expressed both a "want to stay" and "have to stay" in our diversity professional roles.

The difference between a "want to" and a "have to" has much to do with what brought us to diversity work in the first place. For both of us it was clearly a calling—and inward witness that this work was an assignment from God. Believing that God called us to this work, we stayed for as long as we had to. Between the two of us there have been many times when we did not want to stay. Did we mention that this is hard work? We have seen God work even in the midst of hardship. There has been progress on our campuses and within the Christian organizations we have either worked for or worked with. There have been pleasant surprises that have caused our hearts to sing with joy. There have been allies who have accompanied us on our journeys and have helped us celebrate victories large and small and laugh in the face of the resistance that we saw coming a mile away. Through all this we have experienced longevity, earned by learning how to be resilient and to take care of ourselves in both the good times and the hard times. What we have learned about resiliency falls into three categories: self-assessments, support systems, and spiritual formation. We offer our insights as practitioners speaking from a vantage point of longevity.

Knowing Yourself: Self-Assessments

By knowing yourself, we mean understanding yourself on a deep level, recognizing your strengths, weaknesses, beliefs, values, personality, passions, priorities, and triggers. Knowing yourself is a process of self-discovery that requires honesty, deep self-reflection, and a desire to discover who you really are—your true authentic self. This may sound like a strange recommendation. After all, you have been living with yourself all your life. What we are recommending is an understanding of yourself based on developmental tools that can either validate what you think you know about yourself or extend what you know about yourself. Knowing yourself—your true self and your dispositions—will allow you to better leverage your strengths and offer an opportunity to address the areas of your life and work that need attention.

We offer the following assessment tools as suggestions:

- **StrengthsFinder** was developed by a team of scientists and positive psychologists to help people uncover and develop their natural talents. It is within the Gallup family, so a number of other tools that accompany it are useful.
- **Brikman** is an instrument designed to understand interpersonal dynamics through positive psychology in order to achieve higher performance. It is used widely in the fields of career coaching, leadership development, human resources management, and organizational design.
- **Cultural Intelligence (CQ)** is a globally recognized way of assessing and improving effectiveness in culturally diverse situations. It's rooted in rigorous academic research conducted across more than one hundred countries.
- **Intercultural Development Inventory (IDI)** assesses intercultural competence—the capability to shift cultural perspective and appropriately adapt behavior to cultural differences and commonalities. Intercultural competence has been identified as a critical capability in a number of studies focusing on overseas effectiveness of international sojourners, international business adaptation and job performance, international student adjustment, international transfer of technology and information, international study abroad, and inter-ethnic relations within nations.
- **Thomas Kilmann Conflict Mode Instrument (TKI)** allows you to discover whether you might be overusing or underusing one or more of five conflict-handling modes (collaborating, competing, compromising, accommodating, and avoiding), so you can improve how you manage conflict in the future.
- **Workplace Stress Survey** was developed in 1998 by the American Institute of Stress to serve as a simple screening measure to determine the need for further investigation with more comprehensive assessments.
- **Holms-Rahe Stress Inventory** helps you to examine your significant "stress-inducing" life events and correlates the stress load to the probability of illness. In the *Social Readjustment Rating Scale,* the higher the score is, the higher the probability for a stress-related illness.

An added benefit of using assessment tools such as these is that they make great foundations for team building. Having your staff, coworkers, or departments take these as a group will give you common language. In diversity work, having core vocabulary or common understanding of interpersonal dynamics is one of the building blocks for culture change. As an example, in Michelle W.'s third year as a diversity professional, she was able to convince the mosaic diversity team (fifteen individuals from various departments across the university) to take the IDI. After receiving input and training regarding how to utilize the individual and group outcomes to progress the diversity goals, several members took the IDI to their respective teams. After about a year, four departments (student life, human resources, admissions, and adult education) in the university were using IDI language to describe their intercultural interactions with others. After two years, a number of the faculty had taken the IDI and were using the language in their classrooms.

I (Michelle W.) believe some of the major change initiatives that occurred on campus were a direct result of the use of group assessments that helped us develop a common language around our intercultural development. Michelle L. has used the Brikman to assess her own personality and temperament, stress assessments to monitor her level of stress, and both the CQ and IDI as tools for identifying opportunities for inclusion in her professional development plan. As part of my (Michelle L.'s) annual performance review and professional development plan, I include a comparison of assessments from the year prior. The comparisons that show growth are times of celebration. The comparisons that do not show growth are opportunities for self-reflection and further development.

Other Self-Care Practices

Self-assessments are great tools for evaluating a person's emotional, professional, and cultural states. Assessments can reveal the need for further development or the need for some personal restorative practices. A person doesn't always need an assessment to know that he or she is in need of restorative practices, but assessments can confirm the need. When it has been established that restorative practices are needed, we have found the five Cs of self-care a good place to begin: communion, confession, ceasing, community, and care of the body.

- **Communion.** Connecting with God through prayer and med-
  itation. Spending time in God's Word for guidance, assurance,
  encouragement, strength, and healing of emotions. Private silent
  retreats. Private or small-group–facilitated spiritual retreats. Note
  of caution: Leading a spiritual retreat is not the same as being a
  participant. Leading means you are the organizer and facilitator; you are pouring out of your soul as opposed to having your
  soul replenished.
- **Confession.** Sometimes, it's not "them"—it's "us." We are the
  ones who are getting in the way of God's agenda. We are not
  giving our best. We don't have the right attitude. We are not
  prepared. We are not trusting God. In these times, we need to
  confess our shortcomings to God, repent, and make the necessary changes. It is said that confession is good for the soul. We
  agree and would build upon that sentiment by adding that being
  honest with ourselves about the state of our heart, our level of
  energy, our state of mind, and what we have been holding back
  on is not only good for the soul but necessary to flourish in
  this work.
- **Ceasing.** Newsflash, we are not energizer bunnies or Timex
  watches (we might be dating ourselves with the Timex reference);
  we are not designed to just keep pushing through. God created
  the Sabbath for our good. Jesus invited those of us who are weary
  to go to him and find rest. The invitation to stop striving has
  been offered, but we have to accept the invitation. Ceasing looks
  like stopping for a minute to rest and get reorganized. Taking
  a break from the computer screen. Taking a break from social
  media. Taking a break from toxic people and toxic situations.
  Breaks can be as short as five minutes or as long as a year-long
  sabbatical.
- **Community.** We were designed to be in relationship with others.
  Some relationships are intimate and life-long, others are casual
  or short-lived. If it feels like the success or failure of diversity

efforts rely only on you, it could be that you are not sharing the load and that you are suffering from "I got it" syndrome. You may feel like a superhero, but you need people who will help you with the work. You also need people who will support your emotional well-being—you need safe places where you can just be yourself in the company of friends, loving family members, and trusted colleagues.

- **Care of the Body.** You have heard it before, but we will say it here again. Your body is like a car—take care of it and it will take you where you want to go. If you neglect it, sooner or later, you will experience a breakdown. The greater the neglect, the longer it will take to recover—and the more costly it will be to recover. You need to eat right, stay hydrated, get enough sleep, exercise, and make time for play. Caring for your body is important for good health. Don't wait until the new year to make a resolution to do better—make a plan and start today. Your life could depend on it.

In addition to the above-mentioned practices, we also want to recommend regular visits with your doctor. Annual physicals are a must to monitor for developing physical or mental conditions, as well as monitoring known concerns. Attending to our mental as well as physical health is vitally important to our longevity. Often Christians over-spiritualize their mental state and struggle with depression and other mental health issues. This is especially true for marginalized communities who have historically repressed and suppressed trauma in order to survive.

Connecting with Others: Support Systems

Nestled in the book of Numbers (27:1–11), we encounter the story of the daughters of Zelophehad. These sisters give us a wonderful glimpse of biblical solidarity. The law decreed that they could not inherit. They stood up together and approached Moses to contest this unfair decree. What follows is a remarkable story of God's justice meted out to individuals who dared to stand together in the face of systemic injustice.

Most of us know that we need community. However, with the demands of our daily life, sometimes we allow work to disconnect us from the life support systems that truly sustain us. We simply want to remind you to stay connected. Stay connected with family, friends, your inner circle, brothers, and sisters who will call and check in on you periodically, people who are there for you—not your organization, not your department, not your ideas, not your title—just you.

Your personal tribe, your church small group, your inner circle—whatever you call those real people in your life who have your back, those are the relationships you cannot afford to neglect. Because when you doubt or can't remember or get too battered down by the burdens and pressures of this work, those are the people who will stand with you. When you get too overwhelmed by the sheer size of the justice giant in front of you—your brother and sister can remind you of the size of your God. That person standing with you can assure you that we have never seen the righteous forsaken nor his seed begging bread. They can let you know that many are the afflictions of the righteous but the Lord delivers us out of them all!

This is not solo work. We are building community. Community-building *must* take place within relationships, and community needs to be the soil that fertilizes the work. If the community that nourishes you is lacking, you will not have the energy needed to build. It is simple supply and demand. Make sure your cup is filled so you can give out. When your cup begins to diminish, withdraw and fill it up again. This is true for your support system and also for your spiritual well-being.

Deepening Our Faith: Spiritual Formation

> Then, because so many people were coming and going that they did not even have a chance to eat, he said to them, "Come with me by yourselves to a quiet place and get some rest." So they went away by themselves in a boat to a solitary place. (Mark 6:31–32)

Over and over again, we see Jesus retreating to a quiet place to pray. His connection with the Father was vital to his life and ministry. Diversity work is kingdom work. We are fighting supernatural structures and systems that have been embedded in our organizations since their inception. Every day our very presence seeks to dismantle these systems. Please know that you CANNOT do this in your own might and in your own power. The beauty of being believers is that we understand that the battle is not ours but the Lord's. We have to access that power and prioritize the relationship with our source.

It is so tempting to neglect our spiritual selves. Often, we don't even realize when devotions have become routine and prayers have become stale. Prioritizing our relationship with God through daily Bible reading and communion with him is key to longevity in this work. Regular communion with a faith community is another support system. Members of your faith community might also be part of your tribe or inner circle as well.

Being engaged with a worshiping community outside of your organization allows you to refill on a weekly basis. The microcosm that is your campus or workplace cannot be the only community where you worship or fellowship. God is much more diverse than your campus or workplace. Becoming involved in the life of a local church can help you with work/life balance. Suddenly, issues within our organization seem small compared with the challenges of the homeless or imprisoned people your outreach ministry may serve.

The COVID-19 pandemic of 2020 caused almost all worshiping communities to close their doors for months because of federal and state orders to do so in order to slow the spread of the coronavirus. Engaging in worship went virtual for many and for others became a family matter as families quarantined together. During the pandemic, we have heard many say that they have liked the convenience of watching a worship service from their couch or at a time much later than the actual time of worship. Some are declaring that they will not return to physical gatherings—not for health concerns but for convenience. We strongly recommend gathering with others (not just your family) in an organized worshiping community. We are not saying that it must be a large church or even a denominationally affiliated church. We are saying that when it is safe to gather with others, join with others. It can be a small group. We believe the healthiest Christian life is developed in a healthy Christian community. If your church or community is not healthy for your soul, find another one. I (Michelle L.) in late 2020, still in the middle of the pandemic, changed my church membership because the church I had been attending, while good at speaking on the value of prayer, was not good at speaking on the value of Christians being involved in the social justice matters of the day. I felt like my spirit was gasping for air. Through the wonders of technology, I found a church that was both multiracial and spoke of the need of being involved in social justice matters. And not just speaking on it when racial unrest appeared in the news; they had a history of advocating for and leading social justice efforts. The church is forty-five minutes away, so it was tempting for a hot minute to only be a virtual member; but once the doors reopened and I and most of the other members had been vaccinated, I have been present in both body and spirit. There is just something about being with other believers—and gathering together is what God ask us to do in Hebrews 10:25.

In addition to being engaged in a church or faith-based small group, we recommend several spiritual disciplines. Michelle W. is intentional about having a Sabbath day. As an introvert, it is important that she has one day when she's not interacting with anyone. Sabbath days are not spent in church. She writes, reads, listens to music, takes long walks in the park (by herself), and strolls along the beach. She also takes regular retreats and gets massages monthly. She has a scheduled prayer routine, and for the last twenty years she has fasted at the beginning of every year. Perhaps her most centering activity is journaling. Through journaling she worships and communes with God in ways she couldn't if not in written form.

Michelle L. has found reading the liturgies on justice and diversity by Fran Pratt to be restorative. She takes regular spiritual retreats. The retreats occur on a weekday and usually last from 8 a.m. to 8 p.m. No one accompanies her. She takes a journal, a Bible, and music with her. Sometimes she fasts during the retreats; other times she packs light snacks and, of course, plenty of water. She has colleagues who work with a spiritual director. It is something she has thought about. Spiritual direction originated within the Catholic faith tradition. But one need not be Catholic to work with a spiritual director. Spiritual direction is not counseling, and it is not therapy. A spiritual director is a mentor who helps someone more deeply engage their spiritual life and explore their relationship with God.

Takeaways

As we end this chapter, it feels as if we may have been a little preachy. While we are not your mothers (or mamas), we know that very few others will tell you these things. We've found that failure to do these things results in personal crises and leads to burnout and "burn up." We have personally experienced stress-induced illness and can testify that if you do not know and honor your boundaries, no one else will!

4

THE ART OF COLLABORATION ACROSS AN ORGANIZATION

And let us consider how we may spur one another on toward love and good deeds, not giving up meeting together, as some are in the habit of doing, but encouraging one another—and all the more as you see the Day approaching.

—Hebrews 10:24–25

Every organization or institution is inherently political. That is to say, there are a group of people who govern and create and enforce policy. When all is said and done, the politics of an organization center on power, positioning, and status. Rather than repeat our enthusiastic call for strategic allies, this chapter is less about creating alliances and more about "buy-in." How do you get people who are in positions of power to "buy-into" diversity initiatives?

Staff Buy-in

As we've mentioned, one of the reasons diversity efforts fail is because not everyone is following the same playbook. The key to getting "buy-in" is making sure that people know how diversity, equity, and inclusion benefit them. This is especially true for staff members of your organization, those who do the daily leg work; the gatekeepers of administrative spaces, organizational resources, and social capital; the secretaries, coordinators, and assistants; the finance, marketing, and development teams; the residence hall directors and ministry team leaders. These staff members can be even more influential to organizational culture than those who are in the "C-suite."

I (Michelle W.) learned this the hard way in the early days of ministry. As a newly ordained youth pastor, I had "inherited" a group of youth whom I had come to love as assistant youth director. Moving into the primary leadership position felt like an easy transition. However, a particular young man was overly fond of the former youth pastor to the point that he called him to ask for advice or suggestions periodically. *No problem*, I thought. What I didn't know was that he shared all this with a handful of his fellow youth and had established a little circle of them who looked to him for guidance as opposed to me.

After two months of trying to figure out why I had a small coup on my hands, I finally sat down with the young man. I had reached out to the former youth pastor and had asked for his help in curtailing conversations and redirecting them to me. It took a couple of awkward conversations and a little give and take on both of our parts. I promoted the young man to a youth leader and set up regular "check-in" meetings with him. He promised to come to me with questions, advice, and suggestions. Looking back, I can confidently say that although I had the title, he had the influence. I can also attest that sexism and gender role expectations were at work in this situation.

Here's the thing about influence: it is subjective. That is to say, it is *based on or influenced by personal feelings, tastes, or opinions* (Oxford). It can be based upon popularity, beauty, baking, and/or hobbies and interests. One of the most influential individuals in a past job was the lady who baked the best blueberry muffins this side of heaven. She happened to bring them in every week and everyone stopped by her desk to chat and get a muffin. She created a safe space, had a welcoming demeanor, listened well, and fed people. No one wanted to get on her bad side! It also helped that she had significant institutional knowledge and had worked there for twenty years. This is the type of staff member who needs to have buy-in if you want your diversity efforts to flourish.

Much of cultivating buy-in is about "shaking hands and kissing babies." It is intensely relational! It is inviting people to lunch. It is showing you care about them and their concerns. It is praying for and with them. Michelle L. has a story about how cultivating relationships can help create buy-in. I (Michelle L.) was new to my executive level position and had created diversity-focused professional development workshops. Notices went out to all departments informing them of the expectation for everyone to participate in at least one session a year. A member of the facilities team contacted me to ask why that team had to participate in these sessions. In the back of my mind, I was recalling the deep divide between faculty and staff on campus as I explained to him the new requirement, asking if I could meet with him. During the meeting, he asked if I would be willing to meet with a small group of facilities personnel who met regularly for coffee so that I could explain to everyone in the group the reasoning and value of the requirement.

That first meeting led to my being asked to meet regularly with the group and facilitate book studies at their request on diversity topics. However, my greatest joy was when the person who had at first asked me why he had to do this training asked if he could co-lead a session with me for the whole facilities team focusing on structural racism. As a diversity professional, you must position yourself so people feel they can ask you questions and that they have access to you. You have to position yourself so that people from diverse parts of your organization can hear and engage. I cannot tell you how many times I heard, "Wow, never thought a higher-up would have coffee with us." Don't neglect your staff colleagues in favor of trying to "court" those with management and/or executive positions, particularly staff who hold "gatekeeper" positions.

Managing Up

When a diversity incident occurs, it can be a heady thing when the president, bishop, or CEO calls you and not your boss (or when the person calling you is your boss). However, you have to remember this is situational. You cannot burn hierarchical bridges and assume you now have a solid line directly to the "Big Boss." Most of us don't even have a dotted line to the organizational leader; and for those who do have a dotted or solid line to the organizational leader, this doesn't mean that you always have an open flow of communication or are always of the same mind. This means we have to manage our egos and the egos of the person(s) who now finds themself bypassed.

If you already have solid relationships with these individuals, this is easier. However, if relations are tenuous, you need to be intentional about keeping your supervisors informed during crisis. Make sure you copy them on every correspondence. Offer to include them in meetings pertaining to the crisis. Remember that you have to live with these individuals *after* the crisis has passed. These individuals are responsible for your performance evaluations and budget allocations. This is where the Golden Rule comes in handy. Do what you'd like someone to do for you. Be transparent and inclusive. Check your ego.

This applies even more if you do report to the "big boss." Just because they need you right now doesn't mean they always will to this level—you have to manage your expectations during and after a crisis. The truth is that crisis management is a critical part of all our jobs. The fact that none of us anticipates the level of crisis management is irrelevant. It is in our job descriptions.

This doesn't mean that you should not use the demands placed on you and your stellar performance during a crisis as leverage during performance reviews. If you've documented things and kept your supervisor informed, they will know and you are better positioned to request a raise, promotion, or additional funding.

For example, to this day Michelle W. can call the first supervisor she had as a diversity professional and make professional requests because of the relationship that was cultivated during a crisis. She vividly remembers standing in an auditorium after leading a memorial for a student who had just died and being embraced by her supervisor, who said, "You were amazing. I couldn't have done that. I didn't have it in me." It was humbling. It was astonishing. It was the fuel she needed to keep going. There is something about crisis that brings people together. Be conscious of who steps up and stands with you in the midst of crisis. Don't forget to show appreciation and reciprocate when they are in need.

In my role, I (Michelle L.) report to the president of the university. We have a great working relationship that has been tested by a diversity crisis or two. I have been the one called when our campus was in the national news for a racial incident on campus. When called into the president's office, I let him know the work that I was going to have to shift that day so that I could focus my attention on the brewing crises. I have also had an occasion, when asked to take the lead on drafting a written response to a campus newspaper opinion piece, to tell him that I did not have the emotional bandwidth to do so. I informed him that if I wrote the response in that moment, it would not be very Christlike. We could both laugh at that moment. He understood that I was being triggered and that I needed space to deal with my own issues. Being honest about my emotional state and workload is one way I have managed up. Sharing in this way helped him to adjust his expectations for my work.

Being transparent and seeking accountability during a crisis is one of the best ways to garner buy-in with your direct supervisor. It is a matter of establishing trust. If your supervisor trusts that you are not out to sabotage them or their position, then they are more apt to trust your expertise and suggestions regarding diversity work.

Administrators

While staff may have influence and our supervisors write performance reviews, we all know that within all Christian organizations, it is the administration who makes the decisions. Without administrative buy-in, your diversity efforts are doomed. In fact, without wholehearted prioritization of diversity efforts from the senior administration, our organizations will not change.

By administrators, we are referring to C-suite leaders (CEO, CFO, COO), deans, vice presidents, executive directors, presidents, pastors, bishops, and cabinet-level personnel. These are the individuals who allocate budgets and craft strategic plans. In the times in which we live, most of our organizations have some type of diversity statement, goal, or initiative. Most administrators have seen the statistics on demographic shifts and can mentally assent to the need to recruit a more diverse workforce. And as with the others mentioned in this chapter, administrators fall all along the continuum of diversity advocacy. We have both been fortunate to work with administrators who have been supportive of our diversity efforts. By supportive we mean doing more than giving lip service to the value of diversity. By supportive we mean those who are working on enhancing their level of cultural competency and who demonstratively support diversity efforts for the organization. Supportive administrators, especially presidents, are worth their weight in gold. Nothing stops progress on diversity initiatives more than the lack of support from administrators—in particular, the executive level.

One sign of a lack of understanding and support of diversity efforts is when strategic prioritization and budget cuts occur and diversity efforts are among the first to suffer. It seems counterintuitive, doesn't it? So how do we get administrative buy-in that prioritizes diversity efforts? We think it goes back to cultivating individual relationships. Here are a few ways that we have tried to elicit administrative buy-in:

- Meeting with administrators who may, on the surface, appear to be unlikely allies. For example, the chief financial officer and the chief technology officer.
- (For higher education) Host a meeting including the president, vice president for student life, and selected students of color and representatives from other marginalized student groups. These meetings are not for venting but for students to share their experiences, their hopes and fears, and their ideas about what would help them flourish on campus. For example, when Michelle L.'s campus was sending students home during the spring 2020 pandemic, her university president held several virtual town halls with international students who were unable to go back to their home countries. These meetings provided "faces and names" to the numerical description of how many students were still on campus. These informal conversations increased empathy in both directions.
- Host a luncheon for employees of color to share their experiences with senior leadership. Prompt employees of color to be prepared to share their thoughts about how the organization could better live out its commitment to diversity.

- Conduct an organizational climate survey and request an opportunity to share the results and the impact of the results during a senior leadership meeting (and not be last on the agenda!).
- At one of our organizations the provost, the CFO, and the vice president of student affairs sat on the diversity committee. This was *huge* administrative buy-in. We learned together, we discussed hard topics, and we had our pulse on the campus climate. It was a beautiful microcosm of the larger community.
- At our other organization, each of the ten members of the president's cabinet—including the president—meet monthly and individually with the senior diversity professional (who is also a cabinet member). During these meetings, cabinet members are coached on enhancing their personal understanding and practicing of diversity, walking through diversity issues within their divisions, and thinking about possible development opportunities for their staff.

Board of Trustees

The board of trustees is the governing body of most Christian organizations. For churches, this may be a board of elders or council. Generally, the senior leader reports to them. Most of the decision making takes place at the administrative level. However, the board can approve or veto the most significant decisions. The tricky part about getting board buy-in is that diversity professionals don't always have access to these individuals.

In some cases, the organization will intentionally try to recruit diverse board members, although board members are recruited primarily because of their levels of expertise in particular fields or their benefit to the board table. The connection to the organization may be generational (a member of a founder's family), denominational, or financial (a generous donor). Whatever the case may be, this historically has left many of our boards composed of old White men and a few older White women.

The makeup of your organization's board is public knowledge. You should know who is on the board. Some of you will have direct contact with the board via subcommittee and board meeting responsibilities. But the majority of diversity professionals (beginner and mid-level) will not.

So how can we get the board's buy-in when we don't have access? Here are a few suggestions:

- Discover who sits on your board of trustees. One of the trustees could be an old family friend or someone within your network *(true story—a colleague at an East Coast school had no idea that her uncle's best friend sat on the board of her organization)*.
- Boards are always looking to diversify. Don't hesitate to make recommendations to your president if you know of someone who may be a good fit for the board of your organization.
- Suggest a diversity session *(to your senior administration)* as part of board member orientation. At one of our organizations, the orientation session introduces the institution's commitment to diversity, identifies diversity goals within the strategic plan, and introduces the senior diversity professional to new board members.
- Recommend board training. At one of our organizations, the board participates in yearly diversity training. Participation is part of regular board meetings and is mandatory. Training topics are born out of a collaboration between the president and the senior diversity professional. Topics have included the experiences of people of color, cultural intelligence, the case for diversity, and organizational climate survey results.
- Include year-end diversity reports in board packets. Year-end reports vary, but at minimum the report should report changes to compositional diversity—disaggregated by race, ethnicity, gender, and cross-tabulated by role at the organization. By roles, we mean faculty, staff, student, administration, board members, volunteers, ministry staff, congregants, and so on. If a climate survey was conducted in the year, results in summary form should also be included. Ideally, the board packet should include some version of a diversity scorecard or dashboard, as well as progress on diversity goals that are embedded within the organization's strategic plans or a strategic diversity action plan.

- (For higher education) Cultivate a relationship with the president of the student body. Make sure this student is aware of and advocating for diversity issues on campus. If this student is present at board meetings, they can speak to diversity issues from a student perspective. If this student happens to be a member of a marginalized group, then you may have even greater leverage.

Higher Education Context: Faculty Buy-in

Anyone who has been on college campuses for any length of time knows that opposition from faculty can make or break any initiative. Students come to our institutions to study under specific people. These faculty members are the reason many of them choose our institutions. Often they are there much longer than any of the administrators and have established significant credibility within the community. Some faculty are tenured, some are tenure track, and some are adjuncts. Generally speaking, tenured faculty have job security, and if they are resistant to your work as a diversity professional, you will know it and they will feel that they have nothing to lose in expressing their disapproval.

As with everyone else, faculty can fall anywhere along the embracing-diversity continuum. Inevitably, there will be some who will never buy in to anything the organization is doing to try to improve its diversity and inclusion efforts. This is sad but true. The sooner you accept that reality the better. You don't want to waste precious time and energy trying to convert those who don't want to be converted. The "good old boy" system is ingrained and there will be those who will do just about anything to preserve their way of life—yes, even in the sacred halls of Christian higher education.

We say this not to dissuade you from being a champion for the cause of diversity, equity, and inclusion with faculty but to prevent you from unnecessary frustration. These are the matters you commit to prayer as you allow the Lord to break up the fallow ground of deep-rooted, systemic injustice. There will be faculty who are open and receptive. These are the ones you should concentrate your efforts on, the ones who are excited about diversifying their course content and lending their research experience to assist you with diversity efforts. There will also be faculty who are on the fence. There is nothing swezeter than seeing the light bulb go on for one of these particular faculty members in a workshop or training session. It is incredibly rewarding!

Here are a few ways we have tried to elicit faculty buy-in:

- Hosting a special "faculty-only" luncheon with a prominent scholar on a particular diversity topic that is visiting campus.
- Asking a faculty member to lead a workshop or training session based on their expertise as related to diversity. And if they decline the first time, ask again at a later date.
- Strategically inviting departmental faculty to sit on campus-wide programming committees where their research could be highlighted (for example, the foreign language chair sits on the heritage week planning committee).
- Regularly attending faculty meetings, gaining trust, and building relationships.
- Hosting annual "fireside chats" with faculty about classroom and campus diversity issues (intimate meals hosted by the diversity office).
- Talking with the provost and other academic deans about how they have obtained faculty buy-in and implementing those same practices.
- Recruiting faculty members "who get it" to talk with faculty members who are giving you the blues!

Takeaways

Gaining buy-in from staff, administrators, board members, and faculty is not a quick process. It takes time to build trust and credibility. Don't rush the process. Remember to cultivate relationships. Some people will never buy in and the sooner you figure out who those people are, the better. This will save you precious time and energy. Don't let them discourage you from pursuing others. Separate the wheat from the tares and keep moving forward.

TRANSITIONING

> *If any of you lacks wisdom, you should ask God, who gives*
> *generously to all without finding fault, and it will be given to you.*
> —James 1:5

Transition is defined as the process or a period of changing from one state or condition to another. If you think about it, our lives are a series of transitions. We go from childhood to adolescence, teenager to adult, high school to college, working to retirement. Learning to manage our emotions surrounding these various transitions is a part of everyone's life journey.

Transitions are never comfortable. Often they are jarring, disruptive, and exhausting. They take us out of our comfort zones and demand that we be present in two places—the here and the there. Here is the place we know. It is the job that in spite of its chaos, we've come to settle into. It is the students, colleagues, and ministries we love, the office we've decorated, the allies we've cultivated, and the crisis we've averted. However, for most of us the positions we currently hold are not our last.

Statistics on the number of jobs Americans hold in a lifetime are eye-opening—just look at this info from the Bureau of Labor (BLS):

> Individuals born in the latter years of the baby boom (1957–64) held
> an average of 12.3 jobs from ages 18 to 52, according to the U.S.
> Bureau of Labor Statistics. Nearly half of these jobs were held from
> ages 18 to 24. . . . On average, men held 12.5 jobs and women held 12.1
> jobs from ages 18 to 52.[1]

Sometimes transitions are unexpected. Downsizing, position elimination, pregnancies, divorce, marriage, and spouse job change can all impact a person's decision to stay in their job. Whether internal or external circumstances, how we transition is just as important as the decision to transition. "Always leave a place better than you found it." Somewhere along the journey, this phrase stuck with me (Michelle W.). It is a great professional mantra to adopt throughout your career.

Knowing When to Move On

As mentioned above, there are times when transition is "forced" upon you. External circumstances are demanding that you make a change. These transitions can be painful. When the move is the result of organizational downsizing, it is tempting to want to "burn the place down," especially when we did not see the elimination of our job coming. In those moments, we don't want to hear clichés or statements that diminish our pain. While confusion about "what just happened" is to be expected, what we don't often anticipate is the pain of separation or the feelings of rejection that speak to us in the middle of the night.

When this occurs, there is a choice to be made about how we move on. We may not have decided the *when*; but *how* we move on is completely within our control. As the saying goes, "Don't burn your bridges—you might have to cross back over that bridge." I (Michelle L.) have had the uncomfortable experience of deciding how I would write a letter of recommendation for a colleague whose contract was not renewed. It wasn't that I didn't think this person had the skills; it was because the person—on

---

[1]"Number of Jobs, Labor Market Experience, and Earnings Growth: Results from a National Longitudinal Survey Summary," Economic News Release, US Bureau of Labor Statistics, updated October 7, 2020, https://www.bls.gov/news.release/nlsoy.nro.htm.

the person's last day—posted a rather scathing statement about the college on a social media platform and then followed it up with a few disparaging statements about the administration. And technically, I'm part of the administration. Being forced out of a job hurts. The pain and disappointment are real, and it can shake your confidence. Nevertheless, you will get through it. You will survive. You need to move on. Move on without trying to "make them hurt in the same way they hurt you." Move on ready to embrace whatever God has next for you. Move on but maintain relationships with those who have helped you grow in your capacity as a diversity professional.

However, we want to insert a cautionary note here. If you have been forced out of your job unfairly due to discrimination, move on but also consider holding your organization accountable for their wrongdoing. For too many years, the voice of marginalized persons has been silenced. The sad reality is that Christian organizations have been inhospitable and even toxic for anyone that doesn't look, think, or talk like the majority. Recently, two prominent faculty members at the university where I work have resigned, or their contracts have not been renewed. In both cases, there has been media coverage, concerns about structural racism, and cries for accountability. These public headlines are an attempt to bring historically "hushed" matters to the forefront.

Having talked briefly about moving on as a result of external forces, we want to turn our attention to the transition you have personally initiated. Sometimes you have just had enough. There is no amount of money and no title prestigious enough to make up for a toxic environment. If every day you leave work with a migraine and go home to take it out on your spouse and children, *it may be time to move on*. If the stress of your job is causing your blood pressure to continually fluctuate and you are already on medication, *it may be time to move on*. If you have battled for years to push forward diversity initiatives in your organization and haven't seen any fruit from your labors, *it may be time to move on*. If you feel the Holy Spirit nudging, then it is time to move on. These are the manifestations of a restlessness in your soul. Listen to them. They will tell you that it is time to move on. Trust the Spirit to guide you.

Succession Planning

Another professional phrase that has been helpful to us is "Begin with the end in mind." Walking into a new job or opportunity thinking, *How can I recreate myself?* is just a good business practice. Even if you have no intention of transitioning right away, the practices involved in good succession planning will benefit your team. Below are a few suggested practices:

- Make sure your team is cross-trained and that your vision is clearly articulated so that even if you are not there, the work continues.
- Map out organizational diversity goals and post them in accessible places. Goals should be immediate, short term, and long term.
- Communication is key to a successful transition. Meet regularly with your team to update them on current and pending projects. Ask them what they need from you to ensure that things don't get dropped during the transition.
- Don't forget to name the gifts and celebrate your wins with your staff. What have you accomplished during your time? Affirm your team and the good work they've done.
- *Write everything down.* Make sure everything in your head is on paper (electronically and/or physically) and that someone else knows how to access the information so that the next person in your role does not have to start from scratch.

A Transition Story (Michelle W.)

The most impactful transition that occurred for me wasn't my own. It involved a member of my team. We began our positions as coworkers. Then we transitioned to a supervisor–supervisee relationship. This was an interesting transition because I was the supervisor and this individual had been at the organization longer than I. Not only that, but the individual was older and we had developed a friendship I valued.

We worked through the awkwardness of transitioning to a different work relationship and I learned more about myself. Not long after that, the dreaded prioritization conversation began. I was tasked with conveying the news that the above-mentioned individual's position was on the chopping block. This was one of the most difficult conversations I've ever had. The aftermath was even worse. Students were mad, my assistant thought I was the devil, other staff were heartbroken, and I was numb. I had to do what had to be done and tried to lead with transparency. I did my best to communicate with grace and compassion. I prayed, I cried, and I did what had to be done.

I watched as this amazing human being swallowed disappointment and heartache with humility and grace. This individual taught me how to leave well. There wasn't an *i* that wasn't dotted nor a *t* that wasn't crossed. I learned the importance of ritual and celebration. We honored the work of this individual and the impact the position had on the lives of our students and our campus. We allowed space for students, faculty, and staff to lament and grieve. These moments helped us send off our colleague well and also have closure.

Another Transition Story (Michelle L.)

On the first day of my first role as a diversity professional, my boss—the provost—asked me about my *exit plan*. I was perplexed. In my head, I was saying, "I haven't even been on the job twenty-four hours and you are asking me about my exit plan? Oh, this is going to be fun, lol." I had no idea that this question was one of the best I had ever been asked. It is one I didn't revisit for another seven years. After seven years in the role, I was sure that I was done with the job and the college. I had had enough, and I was tired. I was tired of the slow pace of change, I was tired of empty promises, I was tired of the microaggressions, and I was tired of the resistance to change and not being able to push back.

Then that question came back to me: "What's your exit plan?" While I wanted to tell everybody off, thankfully, I made a wiser choice. I decided to move on, but to move on I needed to make sure I was ready to move. I started reading job postings. I made a list of positions that sounded like me and began developing the skills that I didn't have so that I would be ready to move. This process took me about two years. I earned a couple of certifications and designed new programs. I didn't slow down my work even while I was planning my exit. I didn't tell anyone of my plans. My exit plan was to leave for another institution and to be missed by the institution I was leaving.

Then God stepped in. Oh, did I mention that I was praying this whole time? I was praying for clarity, praying to leave, praying for my next job to be better and more fulfilling. God answered my prayers, but not in the way I expected. I did apply for another job and got it—but it was at the same institution, for a newly created executive-level position. It has been the best job I have ever had.

Takeaways

Transitions will occur, perhaps at the same organization. There is an adjustment period with each transition. Pray about what you want. Give yourself grace to adjust. Give yourself permission to grieve. Position yourself for the next chapter in your life. Be open to the unexpected. Give yourself a pat on the back for a job well done.

CHAPTER 6

TO THE DIVERSITY PROFESSIONAL, WITH LOVE

> *As Jesus and his disciples were on their way, he came to a village where a woman named Martha opened her home to him. She had a sister called Mary, who sat at the Lord's feet listening to what he said. But Martha was distracted by all the preparations that had to be made. She came to him and asked, "Lord, don't you care that my sister has left me to do the work by myself? Tell her to help me!" "Martha, Martha," the Lord answered, "you are worried and upset about many things, but few things are needed—or indeed only one. Mary has chosen what is better, and it will not be taken away from her."*
>
> —Luke 10:38–42

It's Monday morning, and as I (Michelle L.) look at my Outlook calendar for the week, there are orange boxes (representing meetings with cabinet members), grey boxes (representing meetings with individuals), black boxes (representing campus committee meetings), teal boxes (representing off-campus committee meetings), green boxes (representing diversity trainings), pink boxes (representing last-minute adds that have not been categorized yet), and purple boxes (representing lunch—when I eat lunch, I usually work through it). When there is a two-hour open window on my calendar, my first thought is *What did I forget?*

We want to encourage you to stop wasting time on people, programs, and polity that do not yield fruit. It may be a good idea, but it may not be a right-now idea. Be strategic and focused about where and how you expend your energy. If we are not careful, we end up running on the proverbial hamster wheel and going nowhere. This is especially true in higher education and churches. The work in these organizations is so cyclical. There is the liturgical calendar, the school year calendar, and the fiscal calendar. There is the regular cycle of an incoming class to enculturate. There are new employees to onboard and old employees to assess. There are annual programs that we are charged with overseeing and revising. There is an ever-growing number of books to read, reports to draft, emails to respond to, assessments to try out, and new policies to adopt. The predictable and unpredictable alike can render us busy—yet noneffective.

We begin resembling Martha. We are doing good work, necessary work. But there is the danger of our motivation and passion for pursuing diversity and inclusion becoming lost among the tasks that seem to never end. We will, as did Martha, cry out, "Lord, don't you see how much there is to do? Can't someone help me!" Or as with too many of our colleagues, we will say, "This is too much! I'm too tired. There's not enough progress—I'm out!" But it doesn't have to be this way. We are proof.

Avoiding Pitfalls

Here we are at the last chapter of Part One: "For the Diversity Professional." There is no way we can capture everything you need to know to be a successful diversity professional within one section of one book. In fact, some things *need* to be experienced in order for you to develop and fine tune your personal leadership and crisis management style.

We mentioned the pitfall of busyness above. Below, we identify the cousins to busyness. By *cousins*, we mean the *effects* of busyness. As we shared above, busyness means we are tending to a number of tasks, big and small; but not all busyness helps us to move the diversity needle. The family name of the cousins is *pitfalls*. Pitfalls are those unexpected dispositions, as a result of unproductive busyness, that create mental roadblocks to creating desired results.

Complacency

This goes along with the point about busyness but should be highlighted. If you haven't changed up your orientation spiel for three years or more, *you may be complacent.* If you use the same illustrations during training that you've been pulling out since you began (and you have been doing this awhile), *you may be complacent.* If you haven't sought out any new data or fresh studies regarding diversity and inclusion, *you may be complacent.* If you haven't reached out to diversity professionals in other Christian organizations (especially those with a different focus) to learn from other practitioners, *you may be complacent.*

How do you fight complacency? Purposefully surround yourself with resources that spark your imagination. Go to a different conference or read a non-Christian author. If you are in the academy, read something written for for-profit businesses. If you are in business, read something written for the academy. If you are at a church or seminary, read something from a different faith lens. Invest in some online training. Travel abroad. Do something to keep those creative juices flowing!

Diversity Superhero Complex

If we are not careful, we can let the weight of the responsibility go to our heads. Just because you are the one everyone comes to when there is a diversity crisis doesn't mean that's the way it is supposed to be, nor does it mean that you are the only one who has to save your organization from the crisis. Sometimes, when an organization is small or when an organization is just launching its diversity efforts, there may be only one person tasked with responding to a diversity crisis.

However, the work of diversity is not limited to designated diversity professionals. Ideally, a lone diversity professional will be able to increase the diversity knowledge and skills of others at your organization so that in times of crisis or in times of needed creativity, a lone diversity professional will not be the only one who is knowledgeable about diversity and inclusion issues at your organization. When you are the only one paying attention to diversity and inclusion, you become the diversity "superhero," saving your organization in times of crisis, fighting the bad guys alone (the resisters or saboteurs), and taking one for the team so that your organization looks good.

We avoid the superhero complex by educating and promoting awareness of these issues so that others can become knowledgeable. This is the foundation of our work. Creating a scenario in which you are the "Be all and end all" may be ego flattering but is unhealthy for you and your organization.

Becoming Bitter

Years of unchecked micro- and macroaggressions can cause anyone to become bitter. We have seen it occur in a few of our colleagues. Guard against bitterness by speaking up when appropriate, having an intimate circle of allies and friends you can vent to, and daily surrendering your life and work to God. Whatever you do, please don't allow bitterness to take root in your heart. If you feel that you are becoming bitter and disillusioned, seek counsel. If you can't shake the bitterness, it may be time for you to move on. Don't hold on to things that are toxic for your soul and poisonous to your ability to conduct yourself in a professional manner. This includes words and people.

Flourishing in the Work

Leading diversity efforts within our Christian organizations is hard work. Sometimes the work is a struggle—struggle to find allies, to see progress, to respond to emails challenging diversity, to find resources, and so on. The struggle is real—nevertheless, so is the possibility of flourishing. To flourish is to grow and develop in an environment that is nurturing and promotes success. Martin Seligman, known as the "founding father" of flourishing, identified five components of flourishing: positive emotion, engagement, relationships, meaning, and accomplishments.

Flourishing is more than simply surviving or "hanging in there." To flourish as a diversity professional means that we are positive about the work we do and about the significance of our work; we view our work as meaningful and so do those around us. To flourish means that we are engaged with the work, enjoy supportive relationships, and experience success in reaching goals. Individual flourishing requires personal well-being, but "new wine" is required for organizations to flourish.

Personal Well-Being

In 3 John 2 we read, "Beloved, I pray that in all respects you may prosper and be in good health, just as your soul prospers" (NASB). This is a pretty good description of personal well-being. How it is experienced may look different from person to person. For example, for Michelle L., good health means a plant-based diet and prospering means making time for rest, spending quality time with family, and ending a day feeling content with what she accomplished. For Michelle W., prospering looks like finding moments of solitude to recharge within the course of a day, having a sense of accomplishment after a long day, and making time for rest, laughter, family, and friends.

Personal well-being will include your self-care practices and spiritual disciplines. There is one other thing we haven't mentioned but feel it is essential to flourishing—*playing*. Have fun, be silly, and laugh out loud. Do this often! Do it at work with your team and your coworkers. Don't be so serious all the time. As Proverbs 17:22 tells us, "A cheerful heart is good medicine, but a crushed spirit dries up the bones." In order to flourish, you will need to find a way to prioritize your soul.

Takeaways

Busyness is a distraction to being strategic. There is *always* something to do, but not everything needs to be done by you. Stop wasting your time on people, programs, and polity that do not yield fruit—sow into people and things that have potential and are bearing fruit. Watch out for mental pitfalls. Flourishing is possible. Remember to play. Personal well-being takes intentionality. Prioritize your soul.

PART TWO

FOR THE OUTLIERS, ALLIES, AND CO-CONSPIRATORS

CHAPTER 7

HELP WANTED

Two are better than one, because they have a good return for their labor: If either of them falls down, one can help the other up. But pity anyone who falls and has no one to help them up.

—Ecclesiastes 4:9–10

Once there were four people named Everybody, Somebody, Anybody, and Nobody. There was an important job to be done, and Everybody was sure that Somebody would do it. Anybody could have done it, but Nobody did it. Somebody got angry about that, because it was Everybody's job. Everybody thought Anybody could do it, but Nobody realized that Everybody wouldn't do it. It ended up that Everybody blamed Somebody when Nobody did what Anybody could have.

It's a clever little story and a reminder, for our purposes here, that you don't have to be somebody with "diversity," "inclusion," or "equity" in your job title or job description to do diversity work. People who have these terms are tasked with setting goals, developing strategies, influencing policy, and leading change within the organization and, of course, the all-inclusive, "other duties as assigned." However, anybody can raise awareness about diversity, inclusion, and equity concerns. Anyone can assist the chief diversity officer or other diversity professional with the work of advancing diversity, inclusion, and equity. True, not everyone brings the same awareness, passion, and skill set; but that's okay. In fact, it's more than okay—it's perfect. Just as there are many parts to the body needed for it to function well, and just as many and varied gifts are needed for the work of the church to function well, there is a need for different kinds of people to advance diversity concerns within Christian organizations.

Who Do You Think You Are?

Not everyone will be a chief diversity officer, just as not all are called to be prophets. Not everyone can be an ally or co-conspirator, just as all are not called to be teachers. Not everyone can be a friend (a true friend), just as not all are called to be pastors. Yet there is a job to be done, and we need those whose vocations focus their energies on diversity, inclusion, and equity—and we need those who are willing to do what they can from where they sit.

Basic Outliers

Outliers are people who don't see themselves as having anything to do with advancing diversity, inclusion, or equity or with helping those designated to do so. They aren't necessarily opposed to the idea of creating or working in a multicultural organization, but sometimes they are. If that's the case, they are more correctly identified as *disruptive outliers*. Basic outliers are people who are either indifferent, don't see a connection between themselves and diversity concerns, or see themselves as not knowledgeable enough to be of help.

Believe it or not, diversity professionals need outliers in their life—at least one or two of both kinds. Disruptive and basic outliers may be of help—they just don't recognize that they are actually strengthening the resolve of diversity professionals and providing valuable insight into what may be the stumbling blocks for advancing diversity. We are not advocating that people stay in their roles of outlier, but truth be told, everybody starts here—but nobody has to stay in this role if they do not want to.

A Friend

Frances E. Kendall has a marvelous essay on the characteristics that distinguish allies from friends and colleagues. Allies can be friends and colleagues, but not all friends and colleagues can be allies. And let's be honest: it is good to have friends who couldn't care less about what we do at work. Our friends are the ones we hang out with for fun, confide in, and who pick us up from the airport at midnight without blinking an eye. Friendships are relationships that can develop at work, but our true friends usually develop outside our work environments. Friends help diversity professionals by assisting them in taking off their superhero capes, so to speak.

I (Michelle L.) met my best friend when I started attending her church. She cares about the work I do, but we never talk about the ins and outs of my job. We (don't judge me) watch Godzilla movies together for the laughs and choreograph dances for worship services (she sings and I dance). It is so refreshing to have her in my life. Our time together always energizes me and reminds me that there is more to me than my work as a diversity professional.

Colleagues

Colleagues are the people we work with within our institutions. They are our coworkers. We may have colleagues who are supportive of our work as diversity professionals, but "supportive of our work" could be simply a matter of mental assent. That is, they may agree that the campus should move in the direction of being more welcoming and inclusive, but they are either not active in helping to transform the institution or they can't provide the kind of support or assistance you need. For both friends and colleagues, there is a relationship that is often positive and affirming, but not in the same way an ally or co-conspirator can be instrumental in helping to transform an organization or being present as a diversity professional works toward bringing about meaningful changes within an organization.

Allies

In essence, an ally is someone who has offered more than their mental assent to helping a diversity professional bring about transformative change. Most people are allies because they know the diversity professional, but others are allies because they have an interest in a particular issue. People who are allies because they know the diversity professional generally like and think well of the diversity professional. They invest their time in building a relationship and see themselves as partners. They have the back of the diversity professional and provide a safe place to raise concerns, vent, and try out new ideas. At times, they are more concerned about the diversity professional as a person than they are about transforming the institution.

People who are allies because of an interest in an issue may be so because of personal experience or an academic interest. They do not see themselves as "friends" with the diversity professional and they are not the people a diversity professional will hang out with or vent frustrations to. This relationship is more transactional. "You scratch my back, and I'll scratch your back." Transactional allies have interest in one or more diversity initiatives. They bring awareness, knowledge, and skills to the table, but their commitment is limited.

Co-conspirators

Darnisa Amante-Jackson, president of Disruptive Equity Education Project (DEEP), says that to be a co-conspirator,

> You understand the historical and systemic implications of race and oppression. You are able to own your privilege and leverage it to say the things that I can't, disrupt the spaces where I still have no "validity" to enter, and agitate the hell out of conversations with white community where I still am deemed "radical." You are okay sitting in discomfort. Co-conspirators know that the absence of something is still something. Doing nothing makes you complicit. Co-conspirators are not complicit; they move with intention. Disruptive intention! They are partnering to end systems of oppression, not to pause them or interrupt like "allies."[1]

Co-conspirators are allies with more skin in the game. They are more concerned about the issue than they are about the relationship with the

---

[1]Cherita Ellens, "A Letter from Our CEO," We-Zine (May 28, 2020), https://womenemployed .org/we-zine-may-2020-issue/.

diversity professional. Co-conspirators are often "partners in crime" with diversity professionals. They are deeply committed to seeing transformative change happen. They often have insight into organizational politics and the culture of an organization. They are, know, or have access to the decision-makers. They know how an organization works and are willing to use what they know to help the diversity professional navigate the organization to bring about transformative change. Co-conspirators often operate as silent partners to the diversity professional. Because they are or are around decision-makers, they are strategically placed to use their influence. With influence they are able to promote a project, explain the benefits of a policy change favoring more inclusion and equity, or speak up when something works against advancing diversity. Because of their access to power, co-conspirators can provide needed cover for diversity professionals when tensions are growing. They can also alert the diversity professional to incoming internal storms so the diversity professional is not blindsided.

It is a luxury to have friends, colleagues, allies, and co-conspirators in your life. It takes time and effort to develop these distinctive types of relationships. But it is well worth the effort and time. We both can say from experience that there have been several initiatives that would not have come to fruition had we not had strong support and sponsorship from an ally or co-conspirator. The fact of the matter is, a diversity professional cannot make deep, meaningful, and lasting change in an organization alone. The organization's broad vision for diversity is at the heart of the role of the diversity professional—but the vision *cannot* be accomplished without the help of friends, colleagues, allies, and co-conspirators.

And so now we ask the question: Who do you think you are? Who are you in your relationship with the person charged with leading diversity efforts at your organization? Think for a moment on the definitions for outliers, friends, colleagues, allies, and co-conspirators. Again, there is good in every role. We are not saying that everyone should or needs to be a co-conspirator. Do the words "If the whole body were an eye, where would the sense of hearing be? If the whole body were an ear, where would the sense of smell be?" (1 Cor. 12:17) sound familiar? There is a need for different kinds of relationships. If you are not happy about who you are, you can change it. But please don't go running to the diversity professional in your life and ask them to recommend what you should do to change your status. We're sure that if you think about it for a while, you can figure it out. And remember: it's not the label that matters. There are no extra stars in your crown because someone has identified you as an ally. What matters is that you show up. What matters is that you provide assistance in a way that is authentic, thoughtful, and helpful.

Gut Check

The Urban Dictionary's definition of *gut check* names the action we hope everyone—outliers, friends, colleagues, allies, and co-conspirators—will pause to do. *Gut check* was "originally a tennis term to describe a player pausing a moment to think about what just happened by closely examining and possibly adjusting his racquet strings. Back in the day strings were made of cat gut, commonly refered [*sic*] to as gut."[2]

We want to encourage you, after completing this chapter, to pause a moment and think about how the things you have read resonate with you. Sharing a Christian faith that believes in a triune God, we ask you to consider allowing the Holy Spirit to interrogate you and to examine your soul. A gut check is not meant to shame anyone or induce guilt; rather, it is an invitation to pause and think about your involvement to promote diversity, inclusion, equity, and reconciliation within your organization; to ask yourself honestly, "Am I who I am called to be?"; to ask yourself, "Is there more I can do?"; to invite the Holy Spirit—the great Helper and source of revelation—to search your heart; and then, after some deep gut checking or soul searching, take a step in the direction toward transformation. Need some help thinking of questions to ask yourself? We offer the following. They are not exhaustive—just a set of prompts to get you started:

- Who am I? Outlier, friend, ally, co-conspirator? What evidence do I have?
- If I were to ask a close friend about who I am, would they come to the same conclusion as I have? If I were to ask the person charged

---

[2]Urban Diction, May 8, 2015, s.v., "Gut check," https://www.urbandictionary.com/define .php?term=gut%20check.

with leading diversity efforts within my organization, would they come to the same conclusion as I have?

- Am I okay with who I am? Why or why not?
- Am I drawn to this work because I want to do it or because I feel I *have* to do it since if I'm not involved, I might be called a racist, sexist, ableist, or something like that?
- What is my "why"? Really, what is *my* "why"?
- Do I know who the diversity champions are in my organization? What do I assume about them? Do I know them because I have a relationship with them or because I have "heard" about what they do or have sat through one of their presentations?
- When was the last time I prayed about my involvement with diversity issues?
- What are my biases? Where did they come from? What steps am I taking to make sure my biases are not hurting my relationships with people in my community, my workplace, and my church?
- What is one thing the Holy Spirit is convicting me of?
- Where is the Holy Spirit leading me?

Regular gut checks are essential for knowing what is really in our hearts and the level of our commitment. They are essential for discerning what we should start doing, what we should stop doing, and what we should continue doing. They keep us grounded, cultivate humility, and lessen the chances of our thinking more highly of ourselves than we ought. Regular gut checks are essential for ensuring that whatever we are doing, we are doing it as unto the Lord.

Takeaways

Diversity professionals need help. Help can come from outliers, friends, colleagues, allies, or co-conspirators. Be cautious about identifying yourself as an ally or co-conspirator. Who you are will be evident by your words and works. It is essential to know who you are and to understand your relationship (if any) to the diversity professional. Regular gut checks are essential.

THANKS! VS. THANKS?

> *Wounds from a friend can be trusted,*
> *but an enemy multiplies kisses.*
> —**Proverbs 27:6**

We've all heard about the caterpillar's transformation process into a butterfly. The process take can up to two weeks. During its transformation, the caterpillar (larva) forms a cocoon (chrysalis) and eventually emerges as a beautiful butterfly. Near the end of its chrysalis stage, the opaque cocoon becomes transparent enough to see the wings. People who are unfamiliar with this process of metamorphosis sometimes believe the butterfly needs help escaping the cocoon. Thinking they are helping, they try to create an opening to make it easier for the butterfly to escape. Unfortunately, the butterfly doesn't need assistance and often dies as a result of human interference. This wonderful natural example gives us a visual regarding what can happen if we try to intervene in ways we think are helpful but are actually destructive. In the next section, we'll speak specifically to some of the ways we've seen "well intentioned" allies and co-conspirators actually hurt the cause. But before we talk about what doesn't help, we will talk briefly about what does help. Specifically, help in the form of help languages. Help languages are words, practices, and behaviors of outliers, friends, colleagues, allies, and co-conspirators who are supportive of a diversity professional.

Help Languages

Similar to Dr. Gary Chapman's "love languages," we believe that different situations and personalities demand different types of help responses.

As an outlier, your primary "help language" may be that of *Courageous Curiosity*. Vocalizing this curiosity in trainings, meetings, and/or email chains is what is needed to move the conversation forward. Often the "elephant in the room" is the question that some are too fearful to ask. I know this is uncomfortable. That is why it requires courage. It also requires discernment. There are appropriate times to ask and inappropriate times. Learning how to "read the room" is a critical skill to develop as a Christ follower. Seeking answers to appease this curiosity in books, trainings, and/ or scholarly resources is a wonderful way to help as well.

One of the most underutilized "help languages" is that of simply *Modeling*. As an ally and/or co-conspirator, using inclusive language, incorporating diverse voices into your curriculum, hiring and promoting underrepresented persons, frequenting businesses that are women- or minority-owned, reading books by authors with a different cultural per-spective, and anything that disrupts the narrative that "White is right" are helpful. Here we are not referring to a "one time" or even during a certain month event. We mean making a practice of it, normalizing these things so that they don't seem foreign or out of the ordinary. If you model "includ-ing" these practices in your daily life, your sphere of influence sees this, *and* those you advocate for and with will see. Just as modeling Christlike love lends credibility to the Christian, modeling inclusive practices lends credibility to the ally/co-conspirator.

Another help language is that of the *Encourager*. This is the person who encourages the diversity professional or underrepresented person or group through words of affirmation, thoughtful deeds, hugs, and praise. The encourager shows up and thanks. The encourager sends emails after the hard meeting and offers thoughtful reflection. The encourager comes by with baked goods and a hug after news of another police-involved shooting.

The encourager affirms the *imago Dei* in every person while standing beside their friend at the protest.

The final help language we will mention is that of the *Giver*. The giver will contribute their time, talent, and treasure to make sure diversity efforts are successful. This individual goes beyond "throwing money" at the issue and is genuinely invested in the outcome. Monetary generosity is one hallmark of a giver, but the investment of time is just as significant.

There are certainly other "help languages" but rather than spend time listing them, we would like to frame them for maximum impact. Just as the effectiveness of the love languages depends on the receiver, so too the help languages. Context matters. You have to know your organization. What works in this context? What works with different diversity professionals? What are the cultural nuances and barriers? The way you've helped in the past may not work right now. It may not have anything to do with you and everything to do with the time and the season. Again, discernment is needed to know if your brand of helping is going to advance, stagnate, or hurt the cause.

When Helping Is Hurting

We begin this section with a quote from Dr. Martin Luther King Jr.: "People with good intentions but limited understanding are more dangerous than people with total ill will." A well-meaning colleague stopped me (Michelle W.) in the hall outside my office years ago. It was mid-February, and Black history month was in full swing. We had just finished a campus-wide chapel service with a rather controversial speaker. I had already felt the rumblings on the walk back from chapel. This well-meaning colleague proceeded to ask clarifying questions on almost everything the speaker stated. After fifteen minutes of standing there, I asked her to schedule an appointment if she wanted to speak further. Then she continued her plea for help and broke down in tears, stating that she needed to process it now because she needed to teach a class, and her students were going to want to process it. She wanted to provide an educated response and not appear ignorant and confused.

This frustrating encounter with a well-meaning colleague was witnessed by several others. Not only did I have to adjust my schedule to deal with her in that moment, but also this interaction sparked White fury because I was labeled "mean and insensitive" toward a beloved professor. The fallout from this one interaction created much more work for me than the actual chapel service. Damage control consisted of refuting a student newspaper article, meetings with faculty, several follow-up meetings with the colleague in question, and a number of student meetings. This is a perfect example of a well-meaning individual who was asking great questions but was centering herself and her needs above all else.

This example highlights the need to examine your motivation as an ally or co-conspirator. We'll discuss this a little later. For now, let's discuss some of the ways unhelpful helping manifests.

White Savior Complex

Well-intentioned White people often wear this complex like a badge of honor. They swoop in to "rescue the poor people" (who are often Black or brown) by digging drinking wells in Africa or building schools in Haiti. Students traveling on mission trips, taking selfies with undernourished children, have become a marker for what it means to be a good "global citizen." This mindset has existed since the founding of this country. Author and historian Jemar Tisby refers back to Christopher Columbus.

> In the mind of Columbus and others, indigenous people did not have the sophistication to develop their own religious beliefs. . . . Instead, they viewed indigenous men and women as blank slates on which Christian missionaries could write the gospel. This paternalistic view of evangelism permeates American church history.[1]

This "let's help them because they are too ignorant or savage to help themselves" attitude is especially dangerous when paired with religious fervor and American notions of meritocracy.

Hyper "Woke" Ally

The above-mentioned incident centered around a colleague of Michelle W. who was (and is) an ally. She wanted to have the "right" answers to give

---

[1] Jemar Tisby, *The Color of Compromise* (Grand Rapids: Zondervan, 2019), 28.

to her students who were looking to her to make sense of a disruptive event (controversial chapel speaker). Here's the challenge with this thinking: She wanted to be the one with the right answers—*even* though she came to Michelle to get her perspective. Basically, she wanted to co-opt Michelle W.'s thoughts and label them as her own. Even if she formed her own opinions and was able to regurgitate them in a nonplagiaristic manner, the motivation to "appear" as if she had all the answers was problematic. The hyper "woke" ally can be harmful if they center the conversation around what they know rather than on the issues being discussed.

Another way the hyper "woke" ally can cause damage is by taking resources or voice away from people in marginalized communities. I (Michelle L.) have had the experience of a White male ally telling me that when the committee I was chairing would go before the president's cabinet to share some of the negative experiences of people of color on campus, he would speak so I wouldn't have to. He told me that people of color should not have to be the only ones talking about diversity. I agree. However, I told him that I didn't need him speaking *for* me, but I would welcome him speaking *with* me. It is frustrating when my voice as a diversity speaker is silenced by a well-intentioned White man. This is not to say that White men don't have anything to say on the subject. On the contrary, we need White men and White women to be vocal and active in assisting in the promotion of diversity and inclusion within our organizations. However, part of doing the work is making sure your own words and actions actually dismantle practices and systems that disproportionately disadvantage marginalized communities and not inadvertently perpetuate the harmful practices. Silencing our voices by speaking for us when we are capable of and desire to speak for ourselves perpetuates marginalization and is not helpful.

When It Hurts to Help

One of the most astonishing things about Jesus is that he intentionally chose to come to the earth clothed in human flesh—fully God and fully human. Isaiah describes the Messiah as "despised and rejected by mankind, a man of suffering, and familiar with pain" (Isa. 53:3). The writer of Hebrews notes, "For we do not have a high priest who is unable to empathize with our weaknesses, but we have one who has been tempted in every way, just as we are—yet he did not sin" (Heb. 4:15). Jesus experienced everything that we as humans experience. He laughed, cried, and felt sorrow, joy, and pain. I believe this is one of the reasons the incarnation was so important. In order for Jesus to be "Emanuel" (God with us), he had to be with us in every way.

There will be times when your stance as an ally, co-conspirator, or friend will hurt. It will hurt because you will feel the pain of the community you are advocating for. It will hurt because you will bleed alongside us. You will mourn when we mourn and weep when we weep. You will lament senseless death and families ripped apart.

There will also be times when you are called upon to physically put yourself in harm's way. This may be via social media. It may be protesting in the streets. It may be with your pen, your art, or your microphone. It may be in a court of law. You may have to spend a night or two in jail after being arrested for protesting. You may lose friends. You may make enemies. You may be labeled "progressive," "liberal," "race-baiter," "gay-lover," "anti-Christian," "heathen," "feminist," and so on. It doesn't matter how prepared you are to face opposition—when it comes, it still hurts.

We want to encourage you to resist the temptation to fix the hurt too quickly. Sometimes we have to sit in the fire for a minute. There are relationships you are just going to have to let go. There are people who will never like you once you align yourself with God's plan for reconciliation. They were fine when you shared the same worldview or just didn't talk about diversity, but when you began speaking up, that was problematic.

There is something incarnational about sitting with people in the midst of shared pain. It is what forges deep bonds. Sitting with the uncomfortable is not natural for many privileged persons. It goes against an ingrained response to "fix the problem." Some problems cannot be fixed right away. The problems of racism, sexism, homophobia, transphobia, tribalism, and so on have been around for centuries. The act of "sitting with the pain" is an act of solidarity. It shows the diversity professional or marginalized persons that you are willing to experience discomfort because they experience discomfort.

It is firmly rooted in the Christian spiritual practice of *lament*, which is defined simply as "a cry directed to God."[2] In our opinion, lament is a needful but seldom-practiced discipline. Emmanuel Katongole and Chris Rice speak of lament in this way: "Learning to lament is nothing less than entering a way of dying to self that is at the very heart of the journey to reconciliation."[3] In experiencing rejection, sitting in awkward and uncomfortable moments, losing friendships, being disowned by family, and/or being ostracized by peers, there is an opportunity to enter deeply into the wounds and hurts of the "other." This process helps us embrace the discipline of lament. According to Katongole and Rice, "To the extent we have not learned to lament, we deal superficially with the world's brokenness, offering quick and easy fixes that do not require our conversion."[4]

I (Michelle W.) will never forget the time when a trusted ally shared her troubled relationship with an elderly relative. She had recently had a "kitchen table" conversation that turned into an ugly argument with name-calling and accusations being hurled. It involved the relative's comments about my ally's gay son. We were able to pray about it and I celebrated with her when she was able to eventually salvage that relationship (after almost a year of hard conversations and silence). A different level of compassion was honed in this ally because of this experience. It was incredibly painful. None of us would choose to walk through painful experiences. However, it is in these dark moments when we see the light of grace more clearly. When it hurts to help, there is a temptation to quit. However, this is the time to remember the transformation of the caterpillar. A butterfly emerges only when the caterpillar pushes through the hard chrysalis.

---

[2] Emmanuel Katongole and Chris Rice, *Reconciling All Things* (Downers Grove, IL: InterVarsity Press, 2008), 89.
[3] Ibid., 87.
[4] Ibid., 149.

Takeaway

Good intentions sometimes have unintended consequences. There are times when this is out of your control. At other times these consequences stem from lack of judgment, discernment, and/or self-centered motivations. As an outlier, ally, co-conspirator, and friend, you must take the time to assess your motives and shepherd your actions. Helping comes at a cost. There is a cost to the people you are helping and to you. Make sure you are willing to pay the cost.

WHO ARE YOU GOING TO BE?

> *Do not withhold good from those to whom it is due, when it is within your power to act.*
>
> —Proverbs 3:27

Most of us know the story of the good Samaritan. At different times, we've all been each of the characters in this story. We've been the individual by the road in need of assistance. We've been the priest and the Levite who saw the man in need of assistance and walked by. We've also been the Samaritan, who stopped, showed compassion, and assisted. When it comes to backing the play of diversity, equity, inclusion, and reconciliation within your sphere of influence, which will you be? Will you be the priest and Levite—or the good Samaritan?

The follow-up question to that is "Why?" Why take the risk? Why be inconvenienced? Why go out of your way to help someone else? Why should you care? Our response is simply because it is the Christlike thing to do. There are moral, ethical, and financial reasons why creating inclusive, equitable organizations should matter to you. But we want to highlight the biblical reason. Listen to these words the apostle Paul pens to the body of Christ: "If one part suffers, every part suffers with it; if one part is honored, every part rejoices with it" (1 Cor. 12:26).

Years later, Dr. Martin Luther King Jr. would echo these words in his speech "Remaining Awake through a Great Revolution": "We are tied in a single garment of destiny, caught in an inescapable network of mutuality. And whatever affects one directly affects all indirectly. For some strange reason I can never be what I ought to be until you are what you ought to be. And you can never be what you ought to be until I am what I ought to be."

Humanity is connected, belonging to one another—stemming from the same source—created in the *imago Dei*. When one person or group suffers, we all suffer!

Your Privilege, Your Calling, and Your Choice

A lot of attention has been given to the term *White privilege.* It is a sociological term coined by Dr. Peggy McIntosh in 1988 in her pioneering paper, "White Privilege: Unpacking the Invisible Knapsack."[1] In her paper, McIntosh describes White privilege as "a set of unearned assets that a White person in America can count on cashing in each day but to which they remain largely oblivious."[2] To be clear, we want to acknowledge that not all outliers, allies, and co-conspirators are White. However, they do all carry some amount of privilege. In fact, we all do. We understand that as middle-class, educated Black women, we have a certain level of privilege. This privilege will get us into places that other people don't have access to and allows us to take advantage of perks that others (even people in our own families) cannot.

This understanding is critical when it comes to leveraging your privilege. I (Michelle W.) can leverage the fact that I have worked with, walked alongside, and befriended some of the greatest theological minds in the world. Therefore, if I am called upon to convene a conference or a think tank regarding theological issues, it would be no problem for me. Others could not say the same. But if I am within their sphere of influence and they are asked to convene a conference, I'm happy to lend my privilege for their cause as well.

---

[1] Peggy McIntosh, "White Privilege: Unpacking the Invisible Knapsack," The National SEED Project, 1989, https://www.nationalseedproject.org/Key-SEED-Texts/white-privilege-unpacking-the-invisible-knapsack.
[2] Ibid.

In general, your privilege is more valuable than you think. Those invisible assets that you take for granted are sometimes the very thing your organization's diversity professional needs. That board you sit on, the connection with the local police department, your husband's golfing buddy, and that florist who would love to do a favor for anyone connected to you—they're all in your invisible knapsack. Take some time to reflect on your areas of privilege that can help strengthen the diversity, equity, and inclusion play within your organization.

We started this book by sharing our stories. We believed it was important to lay a foundation that lets our readers know who we were and our motivation for doing this work. For us, it is a calling. In Chapter Seven we asked you to reflect on your "why." What motivates you to come alongside and partner with those doing this work? Understanding how your unique calling plays into your ally role or co-conspiratorship is vital to sustainability.

I (Michelle W.) mentioned my friend Sarah (not her real name) in Chapter Eight. I met Sarah at a Christian organization where we were colleagues. Sarah's son came out to her as gay when he was twelve. Sarah and her husband pastored a small church in rural America. Her family was outraged and some don't speak to her to this day. Sarah and her husband are still pastors, and her son is still gay. Now at twenty-three, he has a great relationship with his parents and siblings and is currently in graduate school to become a nurse practitioner. After her son came out to her, Sarah discovered she wanted to help other mothers of gay Christian children. She began writing articles and formed a support group. Today that group is a nationwide movement. Sarah found her calling.

The choice to enter into this work and engage on any level is all up to you. We've laid out some reasons we think you should join the cause. However, ultimately, you have to make the decision. If you are reading this book, chances are you already consider yourself an ally or co-conspirator. This is great! We want to help you thrive in this work. We want you to remain in it for the long haul. Every day diversity professionals make a choice to continue to serve on the frontline. Every day you must choose how much or how little you want to engage. The privilege of being an outlier, ally, or co-conspirator is that you get to choose. No one is forcing you to do this. It is not in your job descriptions. There is no written expectation that you will do the work. However, if you choose to engage—do so with your whole heart!

A Call to Action: Look Up, Show Up, Speak Up, Step Up

By now, you've identified who you are. You are either a friend, outlier (basic or disruptive), ally, or co-conspirator. However you choose to identify, now we implore you to act. These are history-making moments. The events that led up to the reenergized civil rights movement that began at the end of May 2020 were painful to live through. Years of compounded rage and anguish erupted on the world stage and none of us were unaffected. In some ways, this is an ideal time for you to act. If you are a newly emerged ally or co-conspirator, there is a momentum that has built, and you can simply ride the wave of that momentum. If you've been at this thing for a while, chances are that you are feeling more hopeful. Like the seasoned diversity professionals you know (and are), you may even be a bit tired, overwhelmed, and/or cynical. However you are feeling right now, it is time to act. It is time to look up, show up, speak up, and step up.

Look Up

"I will lift up my eyes to the hills—From whence comes my help? My help comes from the LORD, Who made heaven and earth" (Ps. 121:1–2 NKJV). The psalmist pens these beautiful words to depict confidence in Yahweh. If we turn our gaze upon him, the Lord will provide the help we need. As you consider deepening your commitment to diversity within your organization, look to your source. God is the one who has called you to pursue this work. God is the one who will sustain you in this work. Turning to God for help when you feel overwhelmed, disappointed, confused, rejected, and ostracized only makes sense. It is quite possible that you won't be able to look to your usual source of comfort for encouragement in this pursuit.

Moreover, you may not be able to look to the diversity professionals or marginalized communities you are championing for support. They may be too tired, too wary, or too busy to act as a sounding board or information guide for you. They may be dealing with so much pressure and stress on their own that the most helpful thing you can do is find another source of comfort and strength.

Finally, in looking up, you set your gaze in the right direction. Often we are so concerned about what is going on around us that all our attention goes to these surrounding issues. Yes, there are awful things going on in the world. However, if we are so consumed with these "earthly things," we risk the chance of missing what is going on in "the heavenlies." Keeping your focus on God through prayer and active listening helps you to stay grounded in your faith and connected to your source. But we caution you to "not be so heavenly minded, that you are no earthly good." Stay grounded in your faith, but don't forget to use that faith as equipping to be an agent of change and renewal in this world (or at least in your sphere of influence).

Show Up

You can't desire to be or call yourself an ally or co-conspirator if you don't show up when diversity professionals or marginalized persons in your organization need you. Trust is developed when you show up. Credibility is strengthened when you show up. Showing up has less to do with what you say and more to do with your presence. Historically, marginalized communities have learned to develop thick skin and limit their expectations because of disappointment by "supposed allies." Please do what you say you are going to do. It may not seem like much to you if you don't show up when you say you will. But believe us—after you have failed to show up, trust is hard to restore. Showing up matters.

Showing up can take many forms. Sometimes it is simply seeing your friendly face in a crowd of hostile faces. At other times, it is your physical presence beside us that counts. Another way you might show up is by helping with planning, setting up, and being the "boots on the ground." You might also show up financially. "Putting your money where your mouth is" is a valid and extremely useful form of allyship. However, if all you ever do is write a check and don't actually engage in another way, this can be seen as "throwing money at a problem."

At times, you may be asked to show up in all these ways. As with so many other things, discernment is needed to determine what form of showing up is demanded in different moments. I (Michelle L.) have always appreciated when people have asked, "How can I show up for you, Michelle; what would be most helpful for you now?" as opposed to people assuming what I need or what would be helpful. However, what makes the ask more meaningful is when someone prefaces their "how can I show up" question with "I can do x, y, or z." What this does is let me know the scope of how someone is willing to show up before I start rattling off possibilities. It also lessens the chances of someone not showing up when they said they would because I have asked them to do something that was outside of their comfort level. Showing up is more than good intentions; showing up takes follow-up.

Speak Up

Much like showing up, speaking up is vitally important in these roles. Silence is not an option for the aspiring ally or co-conspirator. As we watched the unrest and chaos unfold after the shooting of George Floyd in May 2020, we saw this point hit home for several organizations. Suddenly, the Internet was flooded with racial justice statements. Companies you didn't think were invested in the well-being of Black America spoke up. Notable among them were Ben & Jerry's[3] and NASCAR.[4] An ice cream company and a racing organization. If you haven't read their statements and strong stances, we encourage you to do so.

Speaking up when diversity professionals or marginalized persons can't or won't is part of what it means to be an ally. In fact, there are times when the voice of the ally or co-conspirator is the only voice that the "powers that be" will hear. We can't tell you the number of times when a decision-maker has had an "aha" moment after something we've said hundreds of times is said by an ally. Don't be deceived—the messenger still counts. The message may be the same, but sometimes it won't be received

---

[3] "Silence Is NOT an Option," Ben&Jerry.com, 2020, https://www.benjerry.com/about-us /media-center/dismantle-white-supremacy.

[4] "Bubba Wallace, RPM reveal Black Lives Matter paint scheme," NASCAR.com, June 9, 2020, https://hometracks.nascar.com/2020/06/09/bubba-wallace-rpm-reveal-black-lives -matter-paint-scheme/.

unless it is packaged in a certain manner. This does not mean you speak for the diversity professional. In fact, you should strive to amplify the voice of marginalized persons whenever possible.

Step Up

Stepping up means not waiting for someone else to fill the job opening, plan an inclusive hymn fest (singing hymns from different ethnic people groups), or reach out to diverse community leaders, but instead doing it yourself. Even when you know that you may not be the most knowledge-able, be willing to give it your best effort. Even if it means failing the first time you try. Stepping up means raising your hand and trusting your heart to say, "I'll do it! I'll be the bridgebuilder. I'll be a co-conspirator. I'll stop riding the bench. I'm getting in the game." I (Michelle L.) usually facilitate two or more book groups a year. Every now and then, someone will send me an email suggesting a book for my next offering because they would love to read the book with others. My response is almost always, "That sounds like a great book for discussion; why don't you lead it? I'll buy the books and arrange for the room." Sadly, most lose interest and pull back their suggestion. Their idea was for *me* to lead another book group—to add more work on my plate rather than step up and actually do the work themself. Stepping up is more than just offering suggestions; stepping up is doing the work.

I (Michelle W.) love to close trainings with a quote by Rabbi Hillel: "If not you, then who? If not now, then when?" Stepping up is what we've been discussing this entire section. The play has been called and you're up next. Quiet your inner cynic, put on your big boy/girl pants, and step up to the plate. Stepping up is risky. It can feel huge. But stepping up carries with it an eternal weight. Micah 6:8 tells me that "stepping up" is what the Lord requires of me (more on that in the conclusion).

Takeaways

We'd like to end this section a little differently and offer a prayer for those of you who identify as outliers, allies, or co-conspirators:

O God of love and truth, pour out your love on our brothers and sisters. Help them to model love for their neighbor as well as Jesus did. Help them to seek your truth in all things.

O God of justice and forgiveness, may your heart for justice burn within the heart of our brothers and sisters. Forgive them for the ways they've turned a blind eye to those in need.

O God of power and might, may your Holy Spirit embolden them to courageously intervene when they are needed. Grant them boldness to show up and stand up when oppression rears its ugly head.

O God of wisdom, infuse them with your insight. May your Word dwell richly in their hearts, so they may discern when it is time to speak up. Spirit of truth, reveal to them what to say and how to say it so that their words fall on good ground.

O God, be their help, their fortress, their guide, and their peace.

In Christ's name we pray.
Amen.

PART THREE

FOR THE ORGANIZATION

CHAPTER 10

SHARED COMMITMENT

> *I appeal to you, brothers and sisters, in the name of our Lord Jesus Christ, that all of you agree with one another in what you say and that there be no divisions among you, but that you be perfectly united in mind and thought.*
>
> —1 Corinthians 1:10

Habakkuk 2:2–3 is an often-quoted scripture within Christian circles. My (Michelle L.'s) favorite version of this passage comes from *The Message:* "And then GOD answered: 'Write this. Write what you see. Write it out in big block letters so that it can be read on the run. This vision–message is a witness pointing to what's coming. It aches for the coming—it can hardly wait! And it doesn't lie. If it seems slow in coming, wait. It's on its way. It will come right on time.'"

In this passage, God answers the complaints of the prophet Habakkuk. God's response to Habakkuk's lament and complaint about injustice is corrective, gentle, and instructive. Habakkuk had asked God to do something, and God in turn instructed Habakkuk to write a vision so that others can know it, work toward it, and accomplish it. God was telling Habakkuk to develop a shared commitment.

It is not enough for the designated diversity professional or a single senior leader within an organization to have a vision for diversity; no, a vision for diversity must be shared throughout an organization. Ideally, the shared commitment would be something to which *everyone* within an organization has given mental assent, that everyone can articulate in their own words, and that everyone is actively and intentionally seeking to advance within the organization. Good luck with that! As with everything, there is the ideal and then there is the reality. The reality is that not everyone will be actively and intentionally seeking to advance diversity, and not everyone wants to. We talked about this in Chapter Seven, "Help Wanted." The reality is that there are basic and disruptive outliers. Nevertheless, organizations need to be clear about *what* they envision, *why* it matters, and *who* it concerns. Diversity professionals can assist organizations in developing this kind of clarity, but it is important for organizations to own the *what*, *why*, and *who*. When an organization "owns" the vision, they are invested in organizational structure, climate, and outcomes; they invest in evidence-based programming and policies; they practice both internal and external accountability.

What Are You Envisioning?

As diversity professionals and consultants, we have become accustomed to getting "the call" from an inquiring executive, stressed-out program director, or wounded staff member to help them advance diversity initiatives within their organization. The caller usually starts off with an introduction, discloses how he or she got our names and what he or she heard about us, and shares an unnuanced request for assistance with "doing something about diversity" or "leading a diversity training event." (Conversations about compensation, or the lack thereof, come much later). What then follows is an attempt to better understand what the caller is really asking for. For example, when you said, "diversity training," what did you have in mind? Antiracism? Sexual harassment? Knowing your Muslim neighbor? What you should know about your LGBTQ+ student? White privilege and fragility? Cultural intelligence? Diversity 101 for board members? (And yes, we really have led trainings on all these topics).

Sometimes the callers don't really know what they are asking for. They just know they or members of their organization need to grow in awareness, knowledge, or skills. Or they believe their organization needs to or wants to change but doesn't know how to do so. That's okay. Sometimes we don't know what we want. Sometimes we know, but we don't know how to articulate it. And sometimes we know what we want, but what we want is not the same thing that others within the organization want. This is why it is essential to be clear about what is meant by "diversity." Diversity is both a specific term (as would be used by diversity professionals) and a general idea or umbrella term (as is often used by the average person) to collapse the ideas of diversity, inclusion, equity and reconciliation. Collapsing or mashing up the ideas of diversity, inclusion, equity, and reconciliation makes things simpler, but it can lead to frustration when people begin to realize that not everyone using the word *diversity* is saying the same thing. Furthermore, collapsing all these terms creates challenges for understanding what the vision or desired outcome is. Diversity, inclusion, equity, and reconciliation mean different things. Remember that God's instruction to Habakkuk was to be clear about the vision, to be clear about what he wanted. This, too, is our challenge to organizations. Be clear about what your aspirations are. Be clear about whether you are working toward diversity, inclusion, equity, or reconciliation. Be clear about the outcomes you really desire. Below, we define *diversity, inclusion, equity,* and *reconciliation*; highlight the differences and connections between these concepts; and situate each as a diversity level outcome. You might be saying to yourself, *Wait a minute, didn't you just say that collapsing all these terms into one—diversity—could create challenges for understanding vision?* Why, yes, we did. However, what we are doing below is not collapsing terms, but illustrating how these specific terms are related to generalized diversity outcomes. Maybe this example will help. *Acceptable, adequate, satisfactory,* and *superior* are all synonyms for *good.* Two people may be using the word *good* to describe a doctor they are recommending. It makes a difference if by *good* someone means *superior* or *adequate.* If I have a choice, I want the superior doctor. When it comes to diversity, if someone says they are looking to draft new diversity initiatives, the diversity outcomes they seek will depend upon what they mean by diversity. Do they mean compositional diversity, inclusion, or equity?

Diversity

Simply put, *diversity* means "difference." For our purposes here, diversity refers to a collection of people with differing social identities (race, age, gender, sexual orientation, marital status, disability, and so on). We call this "compositional diversity." Help with diversity composition is a frequent request. Other types of diversity include diversity of thought (meaning a variety of perspectives) and intersectionality (meaning the combination of identities that a single person possesses).

As mentioned in our introduction, diversity is something celebrated in the Bible. From the act of creation (Gen. 1) to the fulfillment of the kingdom (Rev. 7:9) to the calling of the first disciples (Matt. 10:2–4) to the calling of disciples today (1 Cor. 9:20–22; Acts 15:19–20), diversity is celebrated and honored. From God's perspective, every person has equal worth and is created in his image. God's Word commands us to love our neighbors as ourselves (Mark 12:31) and to consider others more highly than ourselves (Phil. 2:3). Loving our neighbor and considering others is the way that we should be—especially among Christ followers.

However, we live in a world where sin has corrupted every relationship. And because sin has corrupted relations and social institutions, when speaking of diversity, we need to acknowledge that though our differences do not matter to God, they do matter in our everyday lives. The reality is that some identities are more valued than others. Not fair, not right, not godly—but it's true. If it were not true, we would not have the persistence of gender pay inequity, we would not have had the need for the Americans with Disabilities Act, we would not have the need for the civil rights act, we would not have experienced the May 2020 protests calling for racial justice, and so on. It is a hard truth—especially if you are a person with one or more marginalized identities. When we speak of the plight of people with marginalized identities (stay with me), we *must* also talk about privileged identities. As a reminder, "privilege" is unearned rights and benefits awarded for simply being who you are. Too often privilege is thrown around like an accusation. That is not what we mean or intend here. Here we are asserting the fact that in the United States (and other parts of the world), privileged and marginalized people coexist in every community, in every church, and in every organization. Ignoring that fact doesn't make it not true. Ignoring that fact will sabotage any and every effort to truly promote diversity. *Compositional diversity* is Diversity Outcome Level 1.

Inclusion

Simply put, inclusion is a process of bringing together people and things that are different. For our purposes here, inclusion is the process of incorporating *and* leveraging the compositional diversity that has been attained. Inclusion is more than welcoming. Welcoming is smiling and opening the door for someone to enter. Inclusion builds upon welcoming to incorporate a sense of belonging. When inclusion is cultivated within an organization, marginalized voices and perspectives are sought when decisions (especially those about them) are being made. Both people with marginalized and privileged identities feel that the organization is "their" organization, as if they belong and are equally valued; and "us" and "them" language begins sounding more like "we" and "our." To be clear, we are not talking about assimilation or amalgamation where distinctions are lost, nor do we believe that we are to aspire to assimilation and amalgamation. The end result of inclusion is not a shared single identity or experience.

But wait a minute. Aren't we supposed to have just one identity—as Christ followers? Isn't that what Christ's work on the cross was all about, making us one? Isn't that what he prayed for? Shouldn't we be assimilated into one new identity? After all, isn't that what the Bible says? Take for example "There is neither Jew nor Gentile, neither slave nor free, nor is there male and female, for you are all one in Christ Jesus" (Gal. 3:28).

Well, yes and no. Yes, we are to strive for unity. Jesus prayed that we would be one—meaning unified in our faith and one body as the church. Yes, the work of Jesus on the cross destroyed the dividing walls that separated us. Yes, as people who have accepted Jesus Christ as our personal Lord and Savior, we do share an identity as Christ followers and believers. However, our shared identity must be contextualized. No, we are not to strive to erase our unique social identities. This would be like telling God we no longer want to be who he created us to be. No, although we share the same faith, our experiences related to the faith are different. We are both ordained African American women. We both have friends who are ordained White men. There are some places our White male friends have been invited to preach where we will never receive an invitation to preach—not because we are not known or not good (we are both pretty good—just saying), but because we are both female. To this day, there are still Christian churches that do not allow women to preach from the pulpit, pastor a church, or do anything other than "women's ministry."

So no, we are not yet all one in Christ. Our identities matter to God and our identities influence how we are viewed by our communities and how we experience the world. Denying difference does not equate to inclusion—in fact, it prohibits inclusion. You can't have inclusion without diversity, but you can have diversity without inclusion. You can have a number of diverse people at the table, but those diverse people are simply there to fill a "quota" and don't feel included or valued. We've witnessed both the presence and absence of inclusion in Christian organizations that have identified themselves as "diverse" or "multicultural." *Inclusion* is Diversity Outcome Level 2.

Equity

Simply put, equity is meeting needs in proportion to the need and context. Equity is not the same as equality. The terms are often used interchangeably, but they have different meanings. Both are approaches to achieving fairness, but one takes circumstances and need into consideration, while the other does not. Equality refers to treating everyone the same. Equity, on the other hand, refers to providing access to resources and support in proportion to the need for support and additional resources. For example, a family with two children (one is two and the other is seven) go to dinner at a buffet-style restaurant. There is only one price for the all-you-can-eat buffet: $15 a person. *Equality* would mean that the family of four would pay $60 for dinner. But say the restaurant had three different price points for meals—adults are charged $15, but children under five are charged $2 and children five to thirteen are charged $10. *Equity* would mean that the family's bill for dinner would be $42. In both situations the family has a nice meal and hopefully a nice time. However, the caloric needs and the consumption capacity of the family members are different. In most situations, a family going out to eat would opt for a restaurant that practices equity.

Several Bible passages name equity: "Say among the nations, 'The LORD reigns; Indeed, the world is firmly established, it will not be moved; He will judge the peoples with equity" (Ps. 96:10 NASB1995). "The strength of the King loves justice; You have established equity; You have executed justice and righteousness in Jacob" (Ps. 99:4 NASB1995). "He keepeth the paths of judgment, and preserveth the way of his saints. Then shalt thou understand righteousness, and judgment, and equity; yea, every good path" (Prov. 2:8–9 KJV).

And it could be argued that the early church practiced equity as we read Acts 4:33–35:

> With great power the apostles continued to testify to the resurrection of the Lord Jesus. And God's grace was so powerfully at work in them all that there were no needy persons among them. For from time to time those who owned land or houses sold them, brought the money from the sales and put it at the apostles' feet, and it was distributed to anyone who had need.

We chose to use the New American Standard Bible (1995) and King James Version translations of the Bible in the previous paragraph to present examples of passages using the word *equity*. Other Bible translations use the words *justice* and *righteousness* instead of *equity* in these passages. Justice and righteousness are the essence of equity. Theologians Stassen and Gushee note,

> Most versions of the Bible translate *tsedaqah* as "righteousness," and the King James Version translates *mishpat* as "judgment," so people do not see the Bible's insistence on justice. *Tsedeqah* means delivering, community-restoring justice, and *mishpat* means judgment according to right or rights, and thus judgment that vindicates the right especially of the poor or powerless.[1]

---

[1] Glen H. Stassen and David P. Gushee, *Kingdom Ethics: Following Jesus in Contemporary Context* (Downers Grove, IL: InterVarsity Press Academic, 2003), 345.

As diversity professionals, and more specifically as Christian diversity professionals, we are advocating for equity because of the overtones of righteousness and justice. We also promote using equity as the vision for what an organization wants because equity does not ignore difference; equity embraces difference and seeks to create an environment in which everyone's needs are met, everyone's unique identity is intact and honored, and no one is asked to carry a load that is too heavy for them to bear. Equity takes inclusion a step further by incorporating justice and righteousness. *Equity* is Diversity Outcome Level 3

Bonus: Reconciliation

We are defining *reconciliation* as "compositional diversity + inclusion + equity + faith." Wait—what? Where did that definition come from? From a Christian view, isn't reconciliation the ministry that Christ has given us (2 Cor. 5:18)? Isn't reconciliation about bringing people to Christ and mending broken relationships with one another as the body of Christ? Why, yes, it is. However, we make a distinction between being reconciled to God and being reconciled with one another. Reconciliation with God was made possible by the redemption of our sins as we placed our trust in God. God made us, we rebelled, Jesus paid the price we could not pay (sounds like equity, doesn't it?), we were clothed in the righteousness of Christ and then reconciled with God. Reconciliation with God is the path to salvation.

Reconciliation between people? That takes on different nuances. Reconciliation between people implies that a once-good relationship, broken for any number of reasons, has been restored. We hear many Christian organizations using the term *reconciliation* in association with their diversity efforts. These efforts are generally aimed at increasing the compositional diversity. Efforts such as this are fine for as far as they go. But generally, they are missing something critical. They are missing an exploration of why a lack of diversity exists in the first place. They are missing in-depth conversations about their (historical and/or communal) complicity in the oppression impacting the "other" people. They are missing the fact that the need between marginalized and privileged people is conciliation. Working toward reconciliation without addressing the nature of the breach is like giving someone grapes and asking them to make lemonade. You may end up with a beverage, but it isn't really what you were looking for. It's a pale (or purple) substitute for the real thing. Reconciliation without addressing issues of inequities, exclusion, and lack of compositional diversity is *not* true reconciliation.

Most secular organizations believe that equity is the highest outcome possible for their efforts. We believe that Christians and Christian organizations are called to an even higher standard. That standard is *reconciliation*, but not the reconciliation that is unexamined, not the reconciliation that skips over lament and self-examination, not the reconciliation that protects the comfort of the privileged at the expense of the marginalized and powerless. No, the reconciliation we are talking about and what we wish more Christian organizations championed is that which is grounded in the truth of the gospel while being cognizant of the systemic disparities that sustain the privileged in comfort and relegate the marginalized to oppression. Karl Barth has been credited with advising ministers of the Word to preach with the Bible in one hand and a newspaper in the other. Our advice for people seeking reconciliation is to work toward reconciliation with the Bible in one hand and both a history book and newspaper on your smartphone in the other hand. Of all the diversity outcomes, reconciliation is costliest and the hardest to achieve. It means understanding that compositional diversity alone is not enough, that inclusion still falls short, and that equity is only seeking to be fair, not necessary morally just. It means understanding that reconciliation within the body of Christ is not possible without compositional diversity + inclusion + equity + faith. *Reconciliation* is Diversity Outcome Level 4.

Why Does This Matter?

Understanding your *why* is critical. Your *why* is your motivation for doing the work. The *why* of diversity work for an organization can often be found in its statement on diversity. (What? You don't have one? So what do you think that means? We can help you with that.) Sometimes the *why* is implicitly referred to in founding documents, mission statements, and employee handbooks. There are three primary ways that organizations answer the *why* question: through business, moral and social justice, and biblical mandate.

Business

Why should we do diversity work? Why does diversity matter? Because it makes good business sense. Studies have shown that diversity—diversity in people, diversity in thought, diversity in products and programming—helps the bottom line. Diversity stimulates creativity, extends your reach, improves credibility, and improves productivity (that is, when diversity is leveraged). In fact, McKinsey's 2015 Diversity Matters Report stated that companies with the highest proportions of ethnic and cultural diversity tend to outperform their competitors by over 30 percent. Why diversity? Because it provides a competitive edge. (Read the McKinsey Report.)[2] A business case for diversity speaks to the financial and marketing interests of an organization.

Moral and Social Justice

Why does diversity matter? Why should we do diversity work? Because it is the right thing to do. A social justice case is based on respecting and honoring the humanity of every individual. Morally, as members of the human race, we are obligated to ensure that everyone has the ability to satisfy their basic human needs. No one should be deprived of sustenance, safety, health, love, freedom, purpose, and belonging. Doing diversity work is advancing the cause of social justice. From this vantage point, it is not essential for the "why" of doing diversity work or the answer to the question of why diversity matters to the organization to be grounded in Christianity, or any other faith tradition for that matter. It is simply the right thing to do within a civilized society. The case is made for diversity because people matter.

Biblical Mandate

Why should we do diversity work? Why does diversity matter? Because the Bible tells me so. Unfortunately, individual interpretations of the Bible have been used both to promote and to reject diversity efforts. We won't go into detail here about how select biblical passages have been used out of context

---

[2] Vivian Hunt, Dennis Layton, and Sara Prince, "Diversity Matters," McKinsey & Company, February 2015, https://www.mckinsey.com/~/media/mckinsey/business%20functions /organization/our%20insights/why%20diversity%20matters/diversity%20matters.ashx.

to lead people to believe that the races should be separated, children should not be seen, women should never have a job outside the home, the "crippled" are cursed by God, and nothing should be done to help the poor because they will always be with us and they are lazy. We are pretty sure you know these passages already. We would rather point to the passages and principles in the Bible that we feel promote God's heart for diversity.

A biblical case for diversity is grounded in the command to love our neighbors as ourselves that can be found in both the Old and New Testaments (Lev. 19:18; Deut. 10:19; Matt. 22:37–40; Mark 12:30–31; Luke 10:27; Rom. 13:9; Gal. 5:14; James 2:8). The words of 1 John 4:20 are more direct in their assertion that love of others is vital to what it means to be a Christ follower: "Whoever claims to love God yet hates a brother or sister is a liar. For whoever does not love their brother and sister, whom they have seen, cannot love God, whom they have not seen." We could list other scriptures, but when it comes down to it, the biblical mandate for diversity rests on two ideas: If you love God, you must love the people of God. And you must love your neighbor as yourself. Not just *like,* not just *tolerate,* but *love.* "Love is patient, love is kind. It does not envy, it does not boast, it is not proud. It does not dishonor others, it is not self-seeking, it is not easily angered, it keeps no record of wrongs. Love does not delight in evil but rejoices with the truth. It always protects, always trusts, always hopes, always perseveres" (1 Cor. 13:4–7). If truly practiced, love embraces diversity, demands inclusions, seeks equity, and is most fully expressed in reconciliation. This case for diversity is made because the biblical command to love our neighbors matters.

We have presented three common answers to the question "Why should diversity matter to your organization?" All the reasons present a good argument for making diversity a priority for any organization. For Christ followers, we believe the biblical case is perhaps the most compelling. However, the three cases—business, moral, and biblical—are not necessarily mutually exclusive. It may appear that way because they were treated separately. In practice, organizations have reasons that are mixtures of responses to internal and external crises, personal convictions of change leaders, geographical contexts, and one or more of the three cases that we identified above. While there is no right or wrong answer, if a Christian organization is motivated only by financial reasons, the organization is more driven by profit than by the gospel. Ultimately, which reason an organization chooses is not our decision. Just as the *what* of seeking diversity must be owned by the organization, so does the *why*.

Whom Does This Concern?

Surprise! Working to advance diversity initiatives with an organization is complex. Okay—if you have read this far, you already know that this work is complex and has to be nuanced in order to be effective. There is no one-size-fits-all magic formula or seven-step program to guarantee success or ensure that your organization will never experience challenges and disappointments. (We are working on that book, but it won't be finished until Jesus returns). This is not a reason to throw your hands up in the air and say, "It's not possible, so what's the point?" (Transparency moment: We have both responded this way a couple of times, and it doesn't really help with God's expectation that we follow where he is leading. Conviction is great at getting you back on track with the work you are called to do.) The good news is that when we don't know what to do, we can ask God. If you are not totally overwhelmed by trying to answer the *what* and *why* questions, we have one more question to address before we close out this chapter: "Who?"

Whom is this work meant to impact? This work should matter to whom? The correct answer is *everyone,* right? Right, but there are at least three dimensions to *everyone:* one person, one another, and one organization.

One Person/Individual

"What do you think? If a man owns a hundred sheep, and one of them wanders away, will he not leave the ninety-nine on the hills and go to look for the one that wandered off?" (Matt. 18:12). Every individual matters, and diversity affects every individual. Every individual is a unique combination of identities and experiences. Even for someone who seemingly has only identities that are privileged, diversity (or the lack thereof) still matters for them because their privilege is often under scrutiny. Nevertheless, for most individuals, some aspect of their identity lands them in at least one marginalized category (a person of color, female, LGBTQ+, poor, a person with a disability, and so on). It may not be the whole of their identity, but it is a part of who they are and how they are perceived. Diversity matters to individuals with marginalized identities, especially if they are the only one of their kind within the organization. Being a diversity professional can be lonely (as we discussed in the introduction and Chapter One); being the only one of your kind can be even lonelier. If all but one person in your organization identifies as White, male, able-bodied, cisgender, straight, young, middle class, and Christian, diversity still matters and should be attended to for the sake of the one who is not *and* for the sake of the ninety-nine.

One Another/Interpersonal

"If one part suffers, every part suffers with it; if one part is honored, every part rejoices with it" (1 Cor. 12:26). It can be argued that individuals are created to be in relationship with one another. Relationships are impacted by diversity. In some of the darkest times of US history—the enslavement of Africans, the internment of the Japanese, the boarding of Native American children in schools designed to "kill the Indian but save the man," and too many other policies to name here—our collective relationship with one another was skewed by a failure to see the *imago Dei* in those who did not look like us. This history still affects our relationships today. The legal oppressions, inequalities, and disparities of the past sustain the oppressions, inequalities, and disparities of the present.

Our interpersonal relationships are hampered by residential segregation, school segregation, and monocultural congregations. Our ability to strike up multicultural friendships at work is hindered because of bias in hiring and retention. Even our "friends" on various social media platforms tend to be people who look and think like us. When there is a lack of diversity in our interpersonal relationships, we fail to see that there are other parts to the body of Christ who are not like us. We fail to notice that some parts of the body of Christ are suffering. Diversity matters in our interpersonal relationships. The absence of diversity is an indictment of our failure to see, dwell with, and love our neighbors.

One Organization/Institution

"Where there is no vision, the people perish" (Prov. 29:18 KJV). Organizations are founded with a particular mission. This is their reason for existing. If an organization does not have a vision for diversity, neither will the members of the organization. The people who make up the organization may perish—maybe not in the literal way, but in the sense that the places of work, education, and worship may not reflect their own personal values. Perhaps more distressing, these will not be environments that nurture their souls. Organizations are affected by the presence or absence of a commitment to diversity. Again, by commitment we mean more than a statement found on a website or framed poster in the CEO's or pastor's office. We mean a commitment that is part of decision making, that is spoken of as an essential part of organizational mission, and that can be articulated by every member of an organization. Diversity matters to organizations.

Every organization has been tainted by brokenness as a result of the fall. The hope of God reconciling all things extends to organizations, businesses, churches, and other institutions. It's impossible for two of us (Michelle W. and Michelle L.) and the reader to strengthen the diversity commitment of every Christian organization. Thankfully, what is impossible with us is possible with God. We may not be able to transform every Christian organization, but we can transform the ones where we have familiarity, influence, and membership. We start with the one organization where we have our strongest associations. Starting with our one organization may not rid the world of discrimination based on social identities, but it will improve the Christian witness of our organizations. It will create a more welcoming working, learning, and worshiping environment. And the people will not perish for lack of vision. Diversity matters in our organizations.

Takeaways

It is important to be clear about what is meant by *diversity* within your organization. Diversity could mean compositional diversity, inclusion, equality, equity, or reconciliation. Be ready to answer the question of why diversity matters to your organization. There are multiple dimensions to advancing diversity initiatives: individual, interpersonal, and institutional. How you approach diversity efforts in your organization is a choice, so choose wisely. If fact, choose with a Bible in one hand, and a smartphone with a history book and newspaper app in the other.

CHAPTER 11

SUSTAINED COMMITMENT

Whatever you do, work at it with all your heart,
as working for the Lord.
—Colossians 3:23

Your organization likely has a vision and/or mission statement. Mission and vision statements are the foundations upon which businesses are built and growth is guided. However, often the same thought pattern does not apply to the work of diversity in our organizations. This is a crucial step if there is to be any hope for sustainable change.

We are not suggesting that you draft a theologically weighty diversity statement and stick it on your website and call it a day. This does *not* equate to a sustainable commitment. A written statement is step one. A thorough vision will include a statement, a strategic plan, and a timeline. This is what we mean when we refer to the organization's diversity vision.

As we discussed in the previous chapter, God gave Habakkuk very clear instructions regarding this when he said, "Write the vision and make it plain on tablets, that he may run who reads it" (Hab. 2:2 NKJV). This instruction carries with it an implication that the person or group who is writing the vision is not the one who is actually "running with the vision."

That is to say, the vision is often carried out by individuals in the organization who don't sit around the decision-making table. Therefore, that vision needs to be tested in community.

What do we mean by "tested in community"? When it comes to diversity matters, there is no cookie-cutter formula for how to create sustainable change. The reason for this is simple and has been said multiple times. Every organization is different. Your organizational culture will influence your results. Below we will share general observations based upon years of trends and insights. However, we are by no means trying to be formulaic. What works in one organization may or may not work in another. You have to write the vision, test it in your community, reevaluate, assess, and go back and revise your vision based upon your findings (see our SHIFT model for further details on this).

This *process* must be written into your diversity vision. Our world is constantly evolving. If you haven't revisited your diversity strategy in three years, it's time to do so. Building this into your timeline is important. Having a timeline is crucial. Without a timeline, you don't have measurable benchmarks. Measurable benchmarks are necessary if you are serious about pushing your diversity initiatives forward.

It is important that you do the work of articulating your shared commitment before you engage in the process of crafting a diversity vision. It is also important to allocate enough time to complete the visioning process. Two-day visioning retreats normally barely scratch the surface. Generally speaking, these are more productive if you have an outside consultant leading the process. However, the expectation that your internal team will complete a quality diversity vision document over the course of a two-day retreat is not realistic.

Speaking of being realistic, we should pause and highlight the need for a data-driven, contextually specific vision document. It is great to be aspirational. However, systemic change occurs when organizations address the hard, ugly, embedded, and often unconscious truth. None of this is aspirational. It is realism at its finest. To get to the future you imagine, you have to deal with the past and present you've inherited.

Why Diversity Efforts Fail

As mentioned above, there are no formulaic templates to producing a diverse, equitable, and inclusive organization. Which is to say that there are lots of paths for success. However, this also means that there are also opportunities to fail. Not all failure is bad—failures provide lessons for what not to do when we try again. Note, we said try again. One failure—even an epic failure—does not have to equate to "impossible to achieve." And honestly, we have each had our fair share of failure—initiatives that looked great on paper but did not yield the hoped-for results; an inability to garner the support needed to move an initiative forward; and over-extending ourselves. Failure is part of life. Failure is part of leading diversity efforts and seeking to guide organizational culture change that is meaningful and lasting.

When we fail, *when* not *if*, we pick ourselves up, take a few deep breaths, and perform a postmortem. A postmortem is a set time to review what happened. To look for the reason an initiative failed or to try to determine why achieving a goal is taking longer than anticipated. A postmortem is best conducted with others, especially if the initiative that failed was yours. You need others who can help you see things objectively. You need others who believe in the diversity vision and can help you resist throwing a pity party for yourself. You might need to call a friend to sit with you while you have a pity party, but postmortems are not the time for self-pity or letting your disappointments get the best of you. Wallowing in self-pity robs you of your joy and peace and prevents you from discovering the lessons that will help you be more successful the next time.

With our own experiences in mind, along with what we have observed, we have come up with nine reasons diversity efforts fail. We call these reasons *issues*—as in problems, difficulties, barriers, and roadblocks that undermine flourishing and success. Why do we call reason for failure *issues*? Because we each have had the experience of sharing with a supervisor or co-conspirator that we were having difficulties moving something along and the person responded, "So what's the issue?"

Translation Issues
Inability to translate a need for change and vision for diversity throughout the organization

There are scores of books on change management on the market. This is because change is hard. Organizational change is even harder. If you don't adequately communicate the benefits of the new vision to all levels of the organization, your diversity effort will fail. The key word in this point is *translate.* You must speak the language of your respective audiences. Rolling out a new and shiny vision document that no one understands is ineffective. It must be comprehensible from the janitors to the senior administrators and everyone in between.

Culture Issues
Lack of understanding of organizational culture and what supports it

Senior leadership sometimes presents an idealistic view of an organization and at other times an outdated view of it. While it is true that the foundational bedrock and history of an organization influences culture, organizational culture does morph. External sociopolitical climate, demographic/geographical contexts, and leadership changes have significant impact on organizational culture. If these realities are not taken into consideration when discussing diversity strategies, your efforts will fall short.

Support Issues
Superficial support from senior leadership

Sometimes senior leadership has signed off on the diversity strategies and plans, yet there isn't full buy-in. That is not to say that they don't want to see change. They're just not ready to do what is necessary to facilitate that change. Perhaps they don't have the time or energy to wholeheartedly support the initiatives. If this is the case, your diversity efforts will fail. Senior leadership *must* be 100-percent supportive of diversity efforts. By *supportive* we mean publicly acknowledging, privately affirming, and actively participating in creating culture change.

Investment Issues
Insufficient investment in financial, human, technical, and symbolic resources

Without sufficient resources, diversity efforts will fail. It's as simple as that. For too long, organizations have tried to put "Band-Aid budgets" on diversity efforts. This will not work. You must *invest* in the change you want to see. You must invest time (assessments, community conversations, research into organizational history, etc.). You must invest money (scholarships, hiring, etc.). You must invest in symbols to undo some of the past hurts that are holding back diversity growth (community donations/endowments/sponsorship, inclusive visual displays, memorials, etc.).

According to author and theologian Jim Wallis, "A budget is a moral document."[1] If you allocate more to your university athletics than you do to your diversity efforts, an inherent value statement is being made. The old adage "money talks" applies appropriately in this case. If your diversity budget is one of the first to be cut when you are looking to "trim the fat," an inherent value statement is being made. Whether you realize it or not, this is resistance and will stymie your diversity efforts.

Strategy and Implementation Issues
Symbolic goal-setting with little to no strategy development and implementation

Some organizations are really good at the planning part—but horrible at implementation. They are guilty of "great planning," creating colorful slide presentations stating a renewed commitment to diversity and identifying one or two goals. But that's about all—lots of fanfare but no action. The goals receive only minimal review and strategy development. This is a surefire way to damage your credibility with marginalized communities. You will have trouble retaining high-quality diversity professionals, and your constituents will begin losing faith in your ability to lead. Pretty words and symbolic gestures mean nothing if you do not follow through on what you have planned. In the spring of 2020, a hashtag started trending that speaks

---

[1] Jim Wallis, "Truth That Bears Repeating: A Budget Is a Moral Document," *Sojourners*, March 30, 2017, https://sojo.net/articles/truth-bears-repeating-budget-moral-document.

to this very issue: #meanwhatyousay. Your diversity vision document is no use to you if it's sitting on a shelf.

Framework Issues
Lack of a comprehensive framework to evaluate outcomes of diversity efforts

How do you know if you have reached your diversity goals? If you don't have measurable outcomes, there's no way to track change. Often, organizations underdevelop or overdevelop diversity goals. As a result, you end up with change efforts that fall short of true change. This is why we suggest hiring an outside consultant to help you develop a comprehensive framework. There are some internal blind spots you'll miss if you only rely on internal stakeholders. Internal stakeholders also have unconscious bias toward their "pet" projects, departments, or areas. I (Michelle W.) worked with a client who had previously concentrated diversity efforts and resources solely within human resources. A cursory glance at the makeup of the diversity committee told me all I needed to know. The chair of the committee was the director of human resources, a board member who specialized in employment law was on the committee, and an alumnus who worked in the Equal Employment Office of Compliance also served on the committee. In the end, they discovered that concentrating resources on diverse recruitment, hiring, and employee training was only part of what needed to happen to achieve more than compositional diversity.

Accountability Issues
Failure to establish accountability at all levels

The system of checks and balances helps establish trust within our institutions. Most people bank only with lenders that are insured by the FDIC. Many people eat only at restaurants that have passed a public health inspection and have that certificate visible somewhere in their establishment. Why is this? Because it gives us a sense of assurance that these institutions have met certain standards. Diversity efforts are no different. In order for the constituents in your organization to trust the process, there must be accountability. For the members of your surrounding community to see that you are serious about being more inclusive, there must be accountability. There must be accountability at regular intervals and at multiple levels. For example, you can schedule a three-month goal check in with members of your community to help hold the organization accountable. You can also hold quarterly diversity benchmark sessions with individual departments and supervisors. These accountability measures should be incorporated into your diversity vision document.

Fear Issues
Fear of change and fear of embracing diversity

This is the big one! It actually is the underlying emotion behind some of the other reasons listed. It sounds strange to say that an organization would fear embracing diversity, but it does happen. Fear of embracing diversity shows up as "But we've always been this way—it's our legacy" or "Diversity will start us down a slippery slope toward secularization or relativism" or "We should just focus on our one identity in Christ—all that other stuff is so worldly." Fear of change will stymie any organization's process. The fear may come from board members, donors, staff, community, executives, or all the above. Fear paralyzes us like nothing else can. As members of a faith-based organization, we suggest you go back to the Scriptures and provide a solid biblical foundation for why diversity is a God idea. Faith and fear are not mutually exclusive. I can step out on faith even if I am afraid. The key is—I step out.

Even when you make the faith argument, there will be those who will cling to the fear argument. The "slippery slope" argument is based in fear of change. The fear of change is really about loss of privilege. "If we have to do this, then we will lose that." Systemic injustice is designed to protect those privileges. As an organization, you need to decide where your line in the sand will be. Will you allow fear to derail your efforts or will you step out on faith?

Commitment Issues
Lack of commitment to cultural competency

Unfortunately, you can't just wave a magic wand and become culturally or interculturally competent. You have to unlearn some old things before you can learn new things. This takes time. Time equates to money. Most organizations don't want to invest the time and money it takes to commit to thorough cultural competency training at all levels. It does no good if only your front-facing departments undergo this training. Sustainable change occurs when the entire organization is reading the same playbook regarding diversity matters. Yes, that means everyone from the CEO to the volunteers needs to sit through the same trainings. Please note the *s* on the end of *training*. There is no way that your organization can increase its competency around cultural issues if you don't have a sustained set of mandatory diversity trainings at regular intervals annually. It is short-sighted not to commit budgetary resources to this issue and will result in the failure of your diversity efforts.

Don't Waste a Crisis

It feels slightly Machiavellian to say, but it's true: as an organization trying to move diversity efforts forward, you can't afford to waste a crisis. In this highly visible, tweetable, "Instagramable" world we live in, every organizational crisis needs to propel you forward. If you are under fire for sexist, racist, homophobic practices, you need to immediately address the issues and dedicate resources to prevent similar occurrences in the future. You need to convene with influential leaders within the offended groups to aid you in your "redemption." You need to hire, promote, pay, and *listen* to staff who represent these groups to regain credibility. In short, you need to ride the momentum of the "offensive event" in order to create lasting change. Some donors are more willing to give to stop the bleeding than they are when business is normal. Change happens quickly in the heat of the moment. You just need to make sure you implement long-term, strategic change that is measurable.

Catalytic events hold a mirror up to our organizations and force us to see what is really happening. This is the beauty of a crisis. You can't pretend. You have to face reality. Christians should be familiar with this. The tragedy of the cross is a stark reminder of the ugliness of sin. It is also a beautiful symbol of redemption. The circumstances surrounding a crisis may be ugly. They may be a public relations nightmare. They may reveal things about your organization and the people you employ that you would rather not see. But the beauty of it is that once it is uncovered, it can be redeemed.

Don't Go at It Alone

Organizations are situated within communities. Communities carry the history of the organizations that reside within them. Chances are that your neighbors know as much or more about the history of your organization than you do. Talk with your local civic organizations. Invest resources in developing community partnerships. When a crisis hits, you will need your community partners. When you are looking to advance diversity efforts, community leaders can be some of your greatest allies. Please don't wait until you need community support to develop these relationships. Community partner development should be included in your vision documents. These relationships are critical to your success.

One of the first things I (Michelle W.) did when I became the multicultural director at a midsize organization in the Midwest was to establish a meeting with the local police chief. I wanted him to know me because I was a new professional of color within his neighborhood. I also wanted to establish a relationship in case I needed to intervene on behalf of my students. In that initial meeting, I asked him how we could improve relations with the school. We ended up volunteering at one of the police-sponsored fundraisers. I talked with him about once a quarter and saw him at local events.

About two years after that initial meeting, an African American male student was arrested. One phone call from me to the chief turned a traumatic situation into a teachable moment. This is just one example of how your community partnerships will aid you in your diversity efforts.

Before closing this chapter, we would be remiss if we didn't mention former members of your community. Former employees, students, parents, and board members can be powerful allies in your effort to create sustainable change. They know the inside scoop on your organization. They can give you insight others cannot. Review your exit interviews and look for patterns. Poll your alumni. Periodically reach out to former board members. Work and leverage your networks. You cannot do this alone.

Takeaways

Making a sustainable commitment to diversity efforts was the overall concept of this chapter. According to the Oxford dictionary, *sustainable* is defined as "able to be maintained at a certain rate or level." Your organization now has some incredible insight into why diversity efforts fail and useful tools to help you maintain your commitment at your desired rate or level. We hope you will use them well.

CHAPTER 12

SHIFTING CULTURE

See, I am doing a new thing! Now it springs up; do you not perceive it? I am making a way in the wilderness and streams in the wasteland.

—Isaiah 43:19

Many, many books and articles have been written about organizational culture, some even by Christian authors and for Christian organizations. They claim to be able to help Christian organizations measure and grow organizational culture so that the workplace will flourish. They do this by helping them eliminate toxicity, improving employee engagement, and improving impact. Our purpose here is not to reinvent the wheel or to review every book and article that has been written about organizational culture. In fact, you likely have a few of those books in your office bookcase, on the nightstand in your bedroom, or on your digital book reader playlist (and if you don't, you should). What we want to do here is to simply provide a brief introduction to organizational culture. For a deeper dive into understanding it, we suggest utilizing the services and resources of The

Best Christian Workplace Institute or reading The Culture Factor series from the *Harvard Business Review*.[1]

Sociologically speaking, culture refers to how a group of people make meaning of their collective lives. It includes a mutual understanding of meanings for symbols, commonly held beliefs, and shared values. Culture also includes a shared history and collective identity for the people within the culture. Organizational cultures are the embodiment of goals, values, and beliefs that underlie policies, programs, and social patterns of interaction. The degree to which Christian organizations have an organizational culture distinct from non-Christian organizations is correlated to salience and incorporation of distinctly Christian values and ideologies into an organization's structure and patterns of interaction. Organizational cultures are often set in motion by an organization's founder. The cultural imprint of the founder can last for generations. Much of organizational culture is unspoken. It is pervasive and can be hard to notice until a person is out of the organization and experiences something different. One might not know exactly what it is, but the person will discover it when he or she breaks one of the rules, voices a different understanding, or questions why something is the way that it is.

According to Robert Quinn and Kim Cameron, noted researchers of organizational culture, there are four types of organizational culture: *clan*, *adhocracy*, *hierarchy*, and *market*. The *clan culture* is focused on collaboration and generally see themselves as one big happy family with little friction. Clan culture, not to be confused with "Klan," as in the Ku Klux Klan, is the closest to a functional family-like environment. The primary values are teamwork, communication, and consensus.

The *adhocracy culture* is deeply invested in creativity and energy. Experimentation and risk-taking are encouraged and rewarded. The primary values within this organizational culture are freedom, creativity, and agility.

---

[1] "Resources," The Best Christian Workplace Institute, www.bcwinstitute.org/bcw -resources/; Boris Groysberg, Jeremiah Lee, Jesse Price, and J. Yo-Jud Cheng, "The Leader's Guide to Corporate Culture," *Harvard Business Review*, Jan.–Feb. 2018, https://hbr .org/2018/01/the-leaders-guide-to-corporate-culture.

The *market culture* is based on competition and meeting or exceeding goals (such as a sales-driven culture). Members within this organization understand that success, achievement, and victory are the gold standard.

The *hierarchy culture* is all about control and order. This is the most formal of all the organizational cultural types. Efficiency, certainty, and predictability are the bedrock of hierarchy cultural organization. No organization is wholly one of these types, but rather a mixture of these organization types in combination with the lasting influence of its founders.

Within an organization, culture embodies "the way things are" and "the way we have done things." Organizational culture also creates an understanding of who "we" are and who "they" are, both internally and externally to an organization. Externally, this distinction often originates because of an organization's denominational affiliation. For example, one Christian organization may support same-sex marriage because their affiliating denomination affirms and allows for it. This organization would then likely provide benefits for the same-sex spouse of one of their employees. Another Christian organization, maybe even physically located on the same street, does not support same-sex marriage because their affiliating denomination does not affirm same-sex romantic relationships. This organization would not knowingly hire a person in a same-sex relationship.

Which is the right path? That's a matter for your organization to discuss and decide. As you embark on those conversations, we encourage you to review your organization's mission statement and founding documents, consult denominational statements, examine your employee handbooks to determine what is explicitly and implicitly expressed, and consult with people of differing opinions (ideally with people whose identities represent a range of sexual orientations and identities).

We (Michelle L. and Michelle W.) will not tell you what your policies on same-sex romantic relationships should be, but we will strongly encourage you to be explicit about the "what" of your organization's position and the "why" of that position. This is a conversation that must be had. This is also a matter in which grace and respect should be extended to organizations whose position differs from your own, no matter which side you are on.

Internal to an organization, the distinction between "us" and "them" is dangerous. "Us" and "them" connotes that some people belong and others do not. "Us" and "them" implies a hierarchy that is based upon social identity—especially identities that cannot be changed by effort. "Us" and "them" is fueled by unexamined stereotypes, tightly held biases, and superficial relationships. Superficial relationships are casual acquaintances that seek to "like" other people rather than love them in the way God calls us to love one another. "Us" and "them" within an organization is fertile ground for breeding suspicion, isolation, and discrimination—both subtly and overtly. "Us" and "them" internal to an organization is rarely blatant—at least not in the twenty-first century—but it's always felt. And when it's felt, it doesn't matter how eloquently written a diversity statement is, because the words will mean nothing to the person who feels unwelcome and excluded.

Hallmarks of an Inclusive and Welcoming Organizational Culture

We believe a fair, inclusive, and respectful organizational culture is vital to all individuals and is essential to authentically Christian organizations. It is not enough for an organization to place a welcome mat at the front door and proclaim themselves as welcoming. As pronounced by Jesus in Matthew 7:20, you can tell a tree by its fruit, and in James 2:17 we know that faith without works is dead. Filling your company brochures, church websites, and nonprofit social media feeds with stock images of smiling multicultural groups of people who are not associated with your organization doesn't mean that you are a welcoming organization. And let's not even talk about the repeated images of the two persons of color who used to attend your church, graduated three years ago, or left your organization five years ago. My (Michelle L.'s) son attended a Christian university. Eight years (no exaggeration—*eight years*) after he left, his picture was still on that university's website on three prominent pages. We would joke, but sometimes without much humor, that he should be getting paid or that maybe they thought he was still a student.

Welcoming—and loving, in the way that God has commanded us to love our neighbors—organizations are those that *practice* "welcome."

How do you practice "welcome"? Hospitality. Appreciation. Respect. Trust. Inclusion. Equity. Love. Promoting a culture in which members of the community respect each other regardless of their social identities, their personal histories, their roles within the organization, or the nature of their contributions; fostering a culture in which the welfare of the people—all the people—is prioritized and the flourishing of all is cultivated. Creating a welcoming physical and virtual environment is one that affirms diversity, avoids inappropriate cultural appropriation (too often this is done as an attempt at humor, but it's not funny), demonstrates the value of every person, identifies marginalized people as more than just recipients of services, and points to the ideals of reconciliation. Welcoming churches, nonprofits, and other Christian organizations are those that encourage mutual respect, promote civil and collaborative relationships, and are free from harassment and violence.

Every participant and member of our Christian organizations should have the right to work, worship, and learn in a respectful atmosphere. Promoting and sustaining such an atmosphere is possible only if every participant and member of an organization is expected to abide by values and standards prescribed for interpersonal behavior, communication, and community life. The specifics of such values and standards may vary from organization to organization in the same way that the history, mission, and context of organizations differ—even among Christian organizations. We offer the list below as examples of what could be adopted by your organization. The list is not exhaustive but is a good place to start thinking about what may or may not already be present within your organization. As you review each item on the list, ask yourself, "Is this relevant for my organization?" (Note, we are not saying *comfortable* but *relevant*.) "Is this evident in my organization?" "How do I know?" "Is it explicitly written somewhere in a document or is it just assumed to be true?" "Would the most senior member of our organization feel this is true?" "Would the newest member feel it is true?" "Would members with marginalized identities feel this is true?" "Would members of the numerical majority feel this is true?" "Would people in the community who are familiar with our organization say this is true about our organization?"

- The contributions of all employees are respected and valued, regardless of status or role in the organization.
- Members and participants are treated with respect, civility, and courtesy.
- Members and participants are treated as if they are image-bearers of God.
- Employees work honestly, effectively, and collegially with all others.
- The views and opinions of all are valued and respected, even when differences exist.
- Verbal communication is respectful and courteous.
- People are held accountable for harmful words and actions.
- Disagreements are to be listened to and effectively managed with a hope of resolution.
- The differences that people embody are thought of as assets and not liabilities.
- Cultural differences are respected, and appropriate accommodations are made as needed.
- The use of inclusive language is the default, not the exception.
- Respect for the property and personal interests of those around us, including those of the organization itself, is exhibited.

For those in leadership or supervisory positions, it is important that you model respect and civility for others and clearly define expectations of how members of the organization should treat each other. Leaders and supervisors should also be responsive to all complaints when they are brought forward. Not every complaint will be a crisis; but left unattended, any could indeed become a crisis. Even something that seems like not a very big deal to you means something to the person who brought forth the complaint. Every complaint deserves a response.

One last thing about creating and sustaining a welcoming organizational culture: it is essential to consider intent and impact when designing policy and when responding to a complaint. *Intent* is as it sounds—a hoped-for outcome or purpose. For example, with the intent of strengthening or maintaining the denominational identity of an organization, the organization drafts a policy that all leaders within the denomination must be active members in good standing of a church of that denomination. The hoped-for outcome is that those with decision-making authority will make decisions that reflect denominational policies and align with doctrinal beliefs. Note: there is no malice with this intent. In fact, the intent is to remain faithful. The intent is good. *Impact* is the resulting effect and reaction. Impacts can be intended and unintended. Let's go back to our previous example. The policy has been implemented. People who are not members of the denomination and unwilling to become members of the denomination are not hired nor retained. The intended impact is coming to pass: all leaders are members of the denomination. This is a good thing for churches—you want church leaders to affirm and share theological and doctrinal beliefs.

But what if the organization is not a church and not owned by a denomination and they implement the same policy? An unintended impact could be that there is no diversity among the leadership. If a denomination is not very diverse, that means the pool from which to recruit leaders is also not very diverse. If diversity and inclusion are values and aspirations, this unintended impact works against the stated value of diversity and inclusion.

There's one other unintended impact. Let's say the organization does find a qualified individual of color who is willing to become a member of a local church that is acceptable, but their family is the only family of color within the church (yes, it happens). The unintended impact is that you have inadvertently placed a "minority tax" on this individual. What's a "minority tax"? It's the set of additional expectations and responsibilities placed on individuals in the name of diversity. A minority tax eventually becomes a weighty and heavy emotional, social, and sometimes spiritual price to pay. Being the only one or one of only a couple takes extra work. It takes suffering through microaggressions, being called upon to be the face and voice of diversity even if that is not your job. It takes being called upon to educate everyone else about diversity matters, people assuming and acting as if you are "just like them" and realizing that there are few truly safe spaces for you within the organization. Both of us have been there and done that (that's why we are including it in this book).

As the first "[insert social category]," we knew what we were getting ourselves into. After all, we met the needed qualifications, the hiring manager seemed nice, and this was a Christian organization. At first the minority tax was not too bad. We can deal with it, especially if we feel valued for more than the diversity we bring. Over the course of time, if there are no additional diversity hires, the burden becomes too heavy and plans to leave are underway. And remember what my (Michelle L.'s) momma used to say: "Not everybody smiling is happy."

Here is another example of the difference between intent and impact. A diversity trainer is brought in to lead a professional development training. As part of the training, there is "the invisible knapsack" (also known as the race) activity. The purpose of this activity, based on the essay "White Privilege: Unpacking the Invisible Knapsack" by Peggy McIntosh, is to illustrate White privilege. At the beginning of the exercise, people are asked to form a line, shoulder to shoulder, across a large and open room. The facilitator then recites a series of statements. If the statement is true, you advance one step forward. There are also some variations that have people take a step back if a statement is true, just to mix it up a bit. The statements, between fifteen and thirty, include ones like "I can be late for work and not have it attributed to my race," "When I was growing up, our family owned our home," "I can go to a grocery store and easily find foods that reflect my culture and ethnicity," "When I'm stopped by the police, I can be pretty sure that the officer will look like me and that I will be treated fairly," or "If I ask to see the person in charge, I'm fairly sure that the person will look like me."

The intent is good and the method is both interactive and effective. However, the unintended impact on persons of color can be devastating. Imagine it, because it always happens: you—the lone person of color—are still at the starting line, maybe two steps up, but everyone else has either reached or is in close proximity to the other end of the room. We have heard of times when people of color have broken down in tears during the exercise. I (Michelle L.) will no longer facilitate or participate in "the invisible knapsack" activity. The impact, though unintended, is too painful.

Adding salt in the wound is the witnessing of the privilege of others, the being compelled to share how one felt in the debriefing that follows, and reliving the trauma of being publicly exposed that emerges during this exercise. This is another example of a minority tax at work. The minority tax impact is unintended but nevertheless felt and real. If ignored, it will negate all efforts at developing a welcoming and inclusive culture.

Time to Shift

Healthy organizations are dynamic. At several points in the lifespan of an organization, it will be clear that it is time to shift gears—to make a planned adjustment as part of a strategic plan or to respond to newer technology and changing demographics. If organizations don't make a shift, they become stagnant. If they become stagnant and unresponsive to the passing of time, new technology, and greater knowledge, they quickly become irrelevant and obsolete. For example, changes in technology can connect organizations to wider audiences. During the COVID-19 pandemic in spring 2020, when churches were ordered to close to help stop the spread of the virus, many churches that had not adopted an online presence for worship and Bible study prior to the novel coronavirus outbreak quickly decided to adopt an online presence in order to stay connected with their congregants. Of those that did, many were surprised to see that the number of people accessing their online worship services was greater than the number who were physically present prior to the outbreak. This was true for my (Michelle L.'s) congregation.

The coronavirus pandemic was an unforeseen test of the nimbleness of an organization. Organizations who were dynamic and saw the disruptions to "business as usual" were able to shift resources and priorities to accommodate their new reality while staying true to their mission. Dynamic organizations knew it was time to shift. They may not have wanted to do so, but they felt compelled to do so to ensure their survival during uncertain times. Virtual connections became an added dimension to organizational culture. Because schools were ordered to close out of an abundance of caution, almost every school exchanged in-person class meetings for online virtual classrooms. The change required was immediate. For educational institutions, defining experiences such as athletic events, dorm life, and graduations had to be reimagined. Educational culture was changed, perhaps permanently. For churches, rethinking church membership, pastoral care, and the experience became the subject of church council meetings. Add to this that as many churches have resumed in-person services, some of their memberships have stated that they will not be returning to in-person gatherings, and, if that wasn't enough, many young adults had already begun leaving the church prior to the pandemic. There is a growing concern that some churches will remain permanently closed post-pandemic because they have not been able to or are unwilling to make a shift to adjust to a new reality.

The Coronavirus Pandemic was an unexpected test for an organization's ability to shift to a new reality. However, there is a test currently underway that has been predicted for years in the United States: the demographic shift in the racial and ethnic composition in our nation. In their publication *A Changing Nation: Population Projections Under Alternative Immigration Scenarios*, the US Census Bureau main series estimates that from 2016 to 2060, the US will see a decrease in the non-Hispanic White population by 9.5 percent. However, all other racial, ethnic, and multiple race categories are expected to increase significantly: Black, up 41.1 percent; American Indian and Alaska Native, up 37.7 percent; Asian, up 101.0 percent; Hispanic, up 93.5 percent; and two or more races, up 197.8 percent.[2] The racial shift, when non-Hispanic Whites would become the numerical minority and people of color would become the numerical majority, has been a known possibility for years. The exact year it would happen has been a moving target, but it has been known by demographers since at least the 1970s. Changing numbers nationally will (or already have) manifest in our churches, schools, and businesses. Numbers are one thing; culture is another. Just because an organization has a demographically diverse staff does not mean that an organization has a welcoming and inclusive culture. Diversity and inclusion, as we have said earlier in the book, are not the same thing. Hiring people with historically marginalized identities increases compositional diversity. Having compositional diversity but not valuing nor leveraging diversity leads to only "looking" diverse. Whether as a result of diverse hiring or not, an organization that is intentional about

---

[2] Sandra Johnson, "A Changing Nation: Population Projections Under Alternative Immigration Scenarios," United States Census Bureau, February 2020, Table 5, p. 12, https://www.census.gov/content/dam/Census/library/publications/2020/demo/p25-1146.pdf.

its path of change will more likely become the welcoming and inclusive organization it seeks to be. A welcoming and inclusive atmosphere does not just happen. There must be intentionality.

If an organization's culture is not welcoming and inclusive, *and* there is a desire to be so, a shift in organizational culture must happen. A shift begins to happen when there is an awareness of the need for change. If you think you are good enough or that group is not your market anyway, you may not see the need for change. You may need to do an organizational shift because you are now working remotely, but since there are no people of color in your organization and you don't want them in your organization (even that must be intentional), there is no need to make a shift to become a more welcoming and inclusive organization with regard to race, ethnicity, and nationality. An organization must see the need to change and want to change—to be able to imagine a desired state. Movement from the present state to a desired state can occur only when there is the will to change. The will to change may come from external conditions, such as the 2020 pandemic, or the changes to federal Title IX guidance, or the enforcement of the Americans with Disabilities Act. The will to change may come from an internal push, as in an incoming CEO adding diversity and inclusion goals to a strategic plan or in response to an uptick in employee complaints of racial or sexual harassment and microaggressions. But the will to change can also come from a nudge by the Holy Spirit to shift to more closely resemble God's heart for diversity *and r*econciliation. It can come from a softening of hearts. No matter how it happens, when there is awareness and will, it is time to shift.

SHIFT Components

How do organizations and organizational cultures change? They SHIFT— See, Heighten, Identify, Facilitate, and Transform. In Figure 1, which follows, we provide a visualization of our SHIFT model for organizational change and achieving desired diversity outcomes. The illustration is designed to remind diversity professionals, allies, co-conspirators, and organizations that organizations are defined by mission, situated in a particular context, and impacted by both internal and external social forces.

An organization's mission is its purpose for existence. For example, a university's mission may be to equip students with a liberal arts education so that they can be effective change agents in the world; a church's mission may be to represent Christ in a particular community and to make disciples; a Christian publishing company's mission could be the promotion of the gospel through the printed word; and an adoption agency's mission may be to find permanent loving homes for children unable to stay with their biological families. Mission in this model is the mission of the organization. It is *not* a diversity mission or a diversity statement. Anything an organization does and every policy guiding the organization should be aligned with its mission. All diversity efforts should be aligned with an organization's mission. The context of an organization is the intersection of the historical, geographical, and denominational location of the organization.

Internal or inward social forces are the culminations of motivations, aspirations, internalization, and past successes and failures with diversity efforts. External or outward social forces are the pushes and pulls for change that originate outside an organization. Rushing to shift an organization and its culture without giving thought to mission, context, and inward and outward social forces is like being told to make an article of clothing for someone while having no idea of the person's age, gender, body shape, lifestyle, where the person lives, or what the occasion is. You make a fabulous sequined formal ball gown. It is well constructed. You used a good friend as your model, but when you deliver the article of clothing, you discover that the item of clothing was supposed to be for a five-year-old boy's first day at school.

You may say that sounds a bit far-fetched. But it really isn't when you think about how many organizations are striving for (and failing at) diversity, inclusion, equity, and reconciliation. Organization A has found success in recruiting. Organization B tries to implement the same practices but doesn't have the same level of success. Just as the hypothetical garment was a bad fit and for the wrong occasion, diversity efforts undertaken without consideration of mission, context, and inward and outward social forces are a bad fit—and costly. They cost time, money, reputation— and maybe even the loss of the very people you were trying to retain. We know—we've seen it happen.

We developed our SHIFT model to use with organizations. SHIFT is a five-stage model that is scalable and suitable for organizations of any size or type. We share this model not as a guaranteed formula for success but as a starting place and guidance for the journey. The important thing is to start, to take the first step, and then the next, and the next, and the next until transformation is realized.

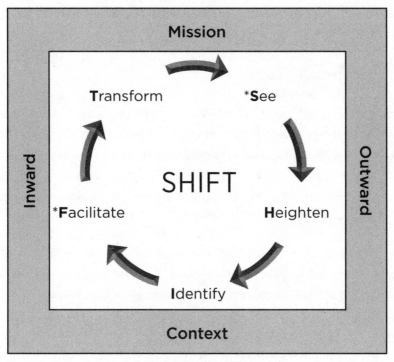

© Loyd-Paige and Williams

Figure 1. SHIFT Model for Organizational Change and Achieving Desired Diversity Outcomes

See—See the Need

Change begins when the need to change is perceived. Seeing the need may originate from noticing that an organization is out of alignment with its mission, the context has changed, or an increased urgency to pay attention to internal and external social forces is realized. An organization may see a need more clearly because the results of a climate survey were not as hoped for; an alarming human resources report shows that in the last year, half of the organization's African American employees left for jobs in other places and there are no people of color in the pool for the organization's one open position; discrimination complaints are on the increase; or the social unrest "out there in the world" is hitting pretty close to home. An organization can also begin seeing the need by talking with its members—the marginalized, the privileged, and all folks in between. An organization can also have its eyes opened to see the need when they earnestly ask the Holy Spirit to reveal the need, to reveal what is breaking God's heart, and to provide guidance on what can be done.

Heighten—Heighten Awareness

Once the need is visible, the next stage in the model is to heighten awareness about current needs and the desire for change. When bringing need into the spotlight, it is important to share only what you have permission to share. For example, as an organizational leader, a person with a marginalized identity may have shared some of their experiences with you in confidence. You are motivated to act and to make things right, so you send out a memo to everyone sharing the details of the event that was shared with you. You didn't provide any names, but everybody knows who the person is. Always ask if and what of personal stories you can share. Personal stories are great for raising awareness and humanizing an issue; but sharing without permission causes reinjury and breaks trust.

Heightening awareness also means making the case for why diversity matters to your organization, obtaining buy-in from key stakeholders, and making public statements about the value of diversity and the kind of diversity outcomes you are hoping to achieve. Heightening awareness is about creating a shared commitment.

Identify—Identify a Plan

The next stage in the model is creating the plan for moving from where you are to where you want to be. Key to this stage is a cultural audit to objectively identify the strengths, weakness, opportunities, and threats of your current diversity efforts. From the organizational audit, goals—short-term and long-term—are developed in alignment with the stated diversity outcomes, as well as the mission and context of an organization. For example, if your church sets a diversity goal to increase the representation of racial minorities to achieve a fifty-fifty mix, this is admirable but could be very difficult if the church is located in a town that is 99-percent White. A better goal to start with might be to increase the cultural intelligence of your congregants by 50 percent. Identifying goals, strategies, and timelines is important but may not mean anything if there is no accountability. We have heard it said: "Diversity is everyone's responsibility." But someone (or a group of people, such as a council) has to have the authority to organize for change and be held accountable when goals are not met (and celebrated when goals are accomplished). When everybody is responsible, nobody is accountable, and somebody is wondering if anything is really changing.

Facilitate—Facilitate Action

Good planning is essential, but without action, all you have is a nicely printed document. Facilitation of the change process is the fuel in the engine. Facilitation looks like the appointment of a person to oversee diversity efforts. It looks like investing in the person who has been appointed to oversee diversity efforts—sending the person to conferences, paying for their skills certification. It looks like creating a budget to adequately fund professional development training for staff and volunteers. And if you are really good, it looks like the most senior leader modeling the importance of diversity-related professional development, advocating for the value of diversity in times when there is not a crisis, and diversifying your circle of advisors.

Note: In the model illustration (figure 1), an asterisk appears beside both *see* and *facilitate*. That's because it's critical that the *see* and *facilitate* are in alignment. The need that is seen can be adequately addressed only if what is facilitated meets the identified need. Otherwise, it would be like staffing a position to facilitate creating a welcoming environment for newly arrived immigrants while the need is for more accessible parking. The solution to a problem is found in the way the problem is defined and understood. Providing a solution based on misunderstanding or misinformation is not really a solution. In fact, it only exacerbates the original problem. We know. We have seen it happen—too many times.

Transform—Transformation through Evaluation

Organizational transformation is the goal, but it is not the final step in the process—because there is no final step. The transformation stage of the model builds on everything that has come before it. The transformation stage is where results are experienced, assumptions are tested, and effectiveness is measured. The three primary activities of the transformation stage are assessment, accountability, and evaluation.

Assessment—you either love it or hate it. You love it because, as the saying goes, "You can't manage what you can't count." When an organization allows accountability, moving from assessment to evaluation will be much more productive.

Through evaluation, organizational leaders are able to identify initiatives that need to be started, fixed, or stopped. When goals are not met, evaluations provide an opportunity to figure out what went wrong and to try again. When goals are accomplished, evaluations invite a celebration for work well done. When goals are met, it signals a time to transition to new goals—to build upon what was learned from the previous set of goals, to address a different set of concerns or a different dimension of diversity, or to transition an organization from diversity outcome level 1 to 2, 2 to 3, or 3 to 4. In many ways, this final stage of transformation is really a transition to a new beginning.

Takeaways

Every organization has a culture. Christian organizations are distinct in their intentional adoption of Christian values and ideology throughout the organization. Organizational culture is highly influenced by its founder and denominational affiliation. Welcoming and inclusive organizational cultures are not automatic, but they can be achieved. It is important to understand the difference between intent and impact. Organizational cultures can and do change. Failure to shift can result in an organization becoming obsolete at best and out of alignment with the will of God at worst. Organizational change is best planned with an understanding of mission and context. The final stage of organizational transformation is really just a new beginning.

CHAPTER 13

CRISIS AND
RISK MANAGEMENT

I have told you these things, so that in me you may have peace. In this world you will have trouble. But take heart! I have overcome the world.
—John 16:33

Regarding difficult times or challenging events, it has been said that a person is either in the middle of a storm, has just come through a storm, or is about to enter a storm. It is a truism that speaks to the individual experience, but it can also apply to an organization. Often the reason an organization begins a diversity initiative is because of a crisis internal to the organization. For example, a letter comes to the president pointing out the lack of accessible parking; an employee makes an allegation of racial discrimination; a student reports an interaction that made them feel uncomfortable; or a vendor is accused of sexually harassing a staff member. Most of these kinds of incidents never make the news, but whether they make the news or not, they still contribute to a perception that an organization is not serious about diversity, inclusion, and equity. When employee and constituent complaints are not addressed, there is a danger of missing patterns of bias and discrimination—either by an individual or by institutional norms. When employee and constituent complaints are always thought to be "overreactions" or "no real harm so no real foul," patterns of complaints and wrongdoing are missed.

Patterns are missed when there is no investigation of a complaint, no tracking of complaints, and no one to whom to submit a complaint. Believe us when we say an organization does not have to put out a neon sign up stating, "We will not be taking your complaints, concerns, and questions seriously." No need for that—it will be known through the grapevine. Organizational leaders like to think that a lack of complaints means that there are no issues; but, again, I (Michelle L.) want to remind you of what my momma used to say: "Not everybody smiling is happy!" A lack of complaints sometimes means that employees don't believe that the place where they work will do anything about their complaints. Nothing will change if they say anything. Trust becomes broken. When people don't trust an organization, they may stay, but they won't be happy. Alternatively, they may simply leave the organization without providing a reason for their unexpected exit. Unresolved internal complaints have the potential of becoming internal storms.

Storms internal to an organization can range from a light drizzle to a category five hurricane, from a minor inconvenience that blows over when cooler heads prevail to major disruptions ending in a lawsuit with the potential to bankrupt an organization. We have both experienced all kinds of storms. Here is an example of what is meant by a "light drizzle." I (Michelle L.) was invited to lead a teacher in-service training event as an external trainer for a school system hundreds of miles from home. The subject was microaggressions. The date was Columbus Day. I invited the teachers to look at Christopher Columbus from a different lens—the lens of indigenous people within the United States. I touched a nerve—a raw nerve—when I brought up the "Adam Ruins Everything" episode regarding Christopher Columbus. A couple of people shared their displeasure and challenged the presentation of Christopher Columbus as anything other than an explorer who brought the gospel to North America. It got a tiny bit heated, but all stayed professional. The next time I led a training for that school system, the resisters from the previous session were very pleasant and engaged, as if there had never been tension between us.

What about examples of category five hurricane storms? For those, you need only to think back to the times when a Christian organization (maybe your own) was featured as an "above the fold" story in a newspaper or featured within the first five minutes of a local or national newscast. We are not here to shame or throw stones. "Love does not rejoice in the wrong" (1 Cor. 13:6—authors' translation).

Not all storms of crisis originate and stay internal to an organization. Sometimes something internal goes viral on social media for all the world to see. Sometimes a lawsuit goes public and, as in our experience, the press has a field day pointing out the fact that something is "not very Christian" about our Christian organization. (Can I get a witness?) When this happens, there is added pressure from outside the organization to do something. External storms are sustained by negative local and national media coverage, trending and unflattering social media posts (and you never see them all—not seeing them all could be a blessing), lack of a timely response, a dismissive posture from senior leadership, and failure to *do something.*

If you are not currently in a crisis or storm, count yourself fortunate. If you have just come through a crisis, take to heart the lessons you learned from the storm and fulfill all the promises made as part of the crisis resolution. If it has been a while since you were in a storm, be forewarned: a storm is coming—maybe internal, maybe external. A crisis is coming. Yet you need not fear the coming crisis or the storms that result. You can prepare in advance and take steps to mitigate the strength of the storm. You can address and resolve minor interruptions before they become major disruptions. (The "how-to" is in the next section—just keep reading.) Crises come because we live in a fallen world. The calls for social justice in the spring of 2020 as a response to a national awakening to the systemic disparities experienced by people of color ushered in a broad sweep of pledges to do better by corporate, nonprofit, secular, and Christian organizations, and people are watching to see if the pledges will be fulfilled.

How are you doing on that front? Was there a promise made, but the emotions of the moment have died down and things are back to business as usual? Have you fulfilled the promises made back then? Then there have likely been more calls for change, and people are watching and waiting. Storm clouds may be forming just over the horizon, but we need not fear the storm, for we know the one who can still every storm.

Crises and Risk Management 101

> A furious squall came up, and the waves broke over the boat, so that it was nearly swamped. Jesus was in the stern, sleeping on a cushion. The disciples woke him and said to him, "Teacher, don't you care if we drown?" He got up, rebuked the wind and said to the waves, "Quiet! Be still!" Then the wind died down and it was completely calm. (Mark 4:37–39)

> Do not be anxious about anything, but in every situation, by prayer and petition, with thanksgiving, present your requests to God. And the peace of God, which transcends all understanding, will guard your hearts and your minds in Christ Jesus. (Phil. 4:6–7)

Headline Stories

Below you will find a few snippets of stories that read like headline news. These are real. They happened to one of us or one of our clients. These situations are not unique to our context—I'm sure some of you could add your own stories. They are just a sampling of things that occur on any given day within Christian organizations.

> The dean of students calls and informs you that an anonymous call came in regarding hazing activities in a male student organization that include potential recruits putting their heads in a noose. Pictures of some of the Black recruits with their heads in nooses have been posted to social media.

> Students are up in arms because of a faculty member's social media page. The faculty member posted strong opinions in support of building Trump's wall and keeping our borders safe from "Mexican thugs" (exact wording from faculty members Twitter account).

A hysterical employee of color comes into the human resources office and reports seeing these words in a bathroom stall: "Barak Obama is a stupid, f**** nig***."

A staff member has recently "come out of the closet" and identified as a lesbian. Her supervisor asked her (without consulting human resources) to be careful about the ways her life intersects with the life of the organization (specifically social media). The staff member shares this information on her social media pages and the organization is immediately labeled as "Anti-LGBTQ Evangelical Christians."

We could go on and on. But you get the point. Not every incident becomes a crisis. Problems arise every day. However, incidents from microaggressions to full-blown crises all carry risks that need to be managed well. Something that starts small or looks insignificant on the surface can blow up into a feature story on the news. And any crises not handled well can escalate into lawsuits. By "handled" we mean finding out what is true, what the perception is, and if there is a way to get ahead of it.

Pre-Crisis Planning

Establish a risk management team. Risk management is the identification, evaluation, and prioritization of risks followed by coordinated execution of resources to minimize, monitor, and control the impact of unfortunate events—large and small. Your risk management team should consist of individuals with the following expertise and oversight: security and law enforcement, human resources, senior administration, diversity professionals, organizational communications staff, event planners, lawyers, and financial resource allocation. The scope of your risk management team will depend largely upon the organization. At the very least, the team should make sure the organization is in compliance with state and federal laws. The team should be responsible for the creation of various crisis management plans that can be implemented in the event of a major crisis. Additionally, this team can be consulted when it is known that something may be viewed as controversial. For example, an employee publishes a book with a provocative title or an invited speaker may be viewed as controversial. In situations like these, the risk management team can count the costs and make a decision to get ahead of the anticipated negative pushback or, in the case of a speaker, uninvite the speaker. This is not to say that an organization has to prevent all potential negative reactions to speakers and books, but it is to say that an organization should count the costs and be prepared for what follows.

Something Has Happened—Now What?

So as an organization, how do you respond to a crisis in the most efficient manner when it hits?

First, you pray. You get centered and ask the Lord for discernment, wisdom, grace, and patience. In James 1:5 we find these words: "If any of you lacks wisdom, you should ask God, who gives generously to all without finding fault, and it will be given to you."

Second, you call your risk management chair and team. You should have identified roles within your crisis management plan for each scenario.

Third, you work the plan. The key to responding well in crisis is pre-planning. This plan should have been authored and approved by the crisis management team.

Here's an example of a solid crisis management plan. This plan can be modified to fit just about any situation.

Act on What Has Come to Your Attention

1. If someone has reported something to you, ensure that they are not in harm's way. If they are in harm's way or are feeling threatened, take action to ensure their safety and peace of mind in that moment. For example, calling the police (if warranted) and offering your office as a safe place. Get the facts and gather evidence. This should happen in minutes, not days.

2. Alert your supervisor, human resource department, or president. Share the facts and concerns. Be prepared to make a recommendation on how to respond. Be clear about what is fact and what is perception. Provide supportive evidence if it exists, such as a screenshot of a photo, a voicemail recording, a copy of a flyer, and so on. In your interaction with your supervisor, human resource department, or president, gain clarity about what your role is. Are you the point person or is someone else? Exhibit clarity about the next steps. For example, it could be that you are to work with someone from communications to draft a public statement; you could be asked to meet with others while members of the crisis management team meet with community members.

3. If you are not the point person, stay in your lane. Don't grant interviews with the media. Don't offer up what you "think" you know to people who are not involved in resolving the problem. You may think you are helping, but you could unintentionally make matters worse. If you are not the point person, you do not know everything that is going on. Stay in your lane. If you have questions, talk to the point person.

4. If you are the point person or if you are working with the point person—

   - **Don't go it alone.** Being the lead person does not mean that this is a solo act. And in times of crisis, you will want to have a team representing various strengths around you and working with you. Proverbs 12:15 cautions, "The way of fools seems right to them, but the wise listen to advice."
   - **Craft a statement.** This initial statement should be simple— something like "We are aware of _____, and we have begun an investigation." Depending on the nature and scope of the event, this statement could be communicated to the reporting party or posted on the organization's social media platforms.
   - **Conduct a very fast analysis of the situation.** What happened? Was there something that led up to the situation? What if any policies have been violated? Who is involved?

What is the reach? What is the actual or potential harm? Who needs to be brought in? Is your organization equipped to handle the fallout? What is the surrounding community's response? What community resources could be helpful?

- **Contact your organization's communications manager** and instruct them to monitor social media feeds and news outlets. Also ask them to be on standby in case they are needed to draft responses in the form of letters, social media outlets, website content, and official statements from senior leadership.
- **Listen** to those who have concerns and who have been hurt by the incidents.
- **Continue your investigation** until you are clear about all the questions raised in your initial analysis.
- **Determine an appropriate response.** Responses could be (1) doing nothing—if responding will only make things worse, doing nothing is an option; (2) initiating informal interventions; (3) initiating formal proceedings as defined in your organization's policies;(4) reporting back and providing an update if someone brought the concern to you.
- **Regroup, rebuild, and refresh.** *Regroup*: Hold a debriefing session with your co-laborers in order to evaluate the process. Review your calendar and take care of things that had to be put on hold as you dealt with the incident. *Rebuild*: Celebrate your successes. What went well and how can you build on that success? Learn from your mistakes. What went wrong with the process, and what can you do to prevent the same mistakes from happening again? *Refresh*: Allow time off for frontline persons to practice self-care. They have been through a lot. Taking care of your staff after a crisis is not optional.
- **Aftercare.** Follow up with all parties involved to check on their well-being and to determine if further remediation is needed. This is also a good time to ask all parties what about the process could have been improved. Shepherding

this process well is what distinguishes the crisis and risk management response of Christian organizations from secular organizations.

This Too Shall Pass

When you are in the middle of a crisis, it can feel almost insurmountable. Trust is broken, reputations are damaged, and progress is stalled at best and undone at worst. It can be hard to believe that your institution will ever recover—or that even you yourself will recover. It may be hard to believe, but recovery *is* possible, and this crisis and storm will pass. Although recovery is possible, it's not guaranteed, automatic, or without great effort. Doing nothing in response to an internal or external originating crisis— hoping, wishing, and praying that it will just blow over and trusting that people will forget if you just ignore it and keep your head down—is an option. It is just not a very good option. It is also not very realistic. People do *not* easily forget. People—especially those who have been wounded, feel marginalized, or are strong social justice advocates—have long memories. In 2007, my (Michelle L.'s) university had a messy separation with a faculty member of color. It made the local and national news. (No, it wasn't me, and I didn't have a part in the matter.) The situation was not handled well, to say the least. The official reason for the separation was that the faculty member "chose" not to renew their contract and had accepted employment at another institution. That was in 2007. As late as 2019 (no exaggeration), twelve years after the person had left the university, the name of the person is *still* being brought up by current faculty and staff as an example of how the university is failing at diversity efforts (their sentiments, not mine.) Could we be doing better? Yes. But are we failing? No. People have long memories. Organizations—deserved or not—develop reputations. The long shadow of bad memories and negative reputations of the past can be hard to escape. Nevertheless, crises do pass. Storm clouds give way to clear skies. Winter snow melts and spring flowers bloom. Regarding each crisis big and small—this too shall pass.

However, as it was for the Israelites escaping bondage in Egypt, our attitude and actions will determine the duration of the journey (recovery time) and who survives the journey. Yes, this too shall pass—but will it be a seven-day journey or a forty-year journey? Will it be a journey of redemption and healing or one of loss and aggravation? The previous section—"Crises and Risk Management 101"—provides a path for navigating internal and external crises when they arise. However, preventative measures can be taken to lessen the impact of coming storms. Listening to and taking seriously the critique of diversity policies, attending to complaints about discrimination and harassment, and not waiting until there is a crisis to make changes in organizational culture are simple preventative steps that can be taken before a light drizzle of inconvenience turns into a catastrophic category five hurricane. Crises big and small will pass, but how and when they pass is determined by the actions, or lack of actions, by your organization, its leaders, and its members.

Takeaways

Organizations are either in the middle of a diversity-related storm, about to enter a storm, or have recently exited a storm generated by an internal or external crisis. It can happen to any organization. Christian organizations are not exempt from mishandling a situation. Having a risk and crisis management plan in place before a storm hits is preferable. If crises are not adequately addressed, the long shadows of bad memories and negative reputations will impact future efforts. Crises are not fun to experience, but they will eventually pass.

CHAPTER 14

WHAT DOES SUCCESS LOOK LIKE?

> *But he's already made it plain how to live, what to do, what GOD*
> *is looking for in men and women. It's quite simple: Do what is fair*
> *and just to your neighbor, be compassionate and loyal in your love,*
> *And don't take yourself too seriously—take GOD seriously.*
>
> —Micah 6:8 *The Message*

Even with clarity of your "why," "what," and "who" of diversity work, desired outcomes do not always happen. This can be disappointing. You had high hopes and aspirations. You wrote the vision and made it plain. You *saw* the need, *heightened* awareness, *identified* where you are and where you want to be, and *facilitated* the process. Prayers were uttered, voices were raised, tears were cried, and compromises were made. Allies and co-conspirators were located and engaged. But where's the *transformation*? You kicked off the year with a catchy slogan, obtained buy-in from key stakeholders, met every week with the diversity implementation team for nearly a year (but it feels so much longer than that); nevertheless, your organization has yet to achieve *Level 1 outcomes*. You were sure you would be transitioning from *Level 2* to *Level 3 outcomes* by now, maybe even on the verge of engaging *Level 4*. You followed the SHIFT model and engaged a pricey consultant, and for all of this it seems that hardly anything was accomplished. We know: we have seen it before. We have not only seen it but also lived it—still living it if we are honest. If this is your reality, we offer this word of assurance: even the best organizations—Christian and non-Christian alike—struggle with achieving their most ambitious diversity goals. Wise organizations and diversity professionals understand that the work of transforming organizations is a marathon, not a sprint, and that in the end it's about progress, not perfection.

"Progress, not perfection" can sound like excuse-making or a euphemism for covering up lack of commitment and effort. And, truth be told, yes, some are making excuses for a lack of effort. But we sincerely believe and know from experience that change doesn't happen overnight. The fruit resulting from changed policies may not appear for a couple of years. It takes time. The expected changed behavior anticipated from mandated antibias professional development training is manifesting quickly in some lives and has yet to be seen in others. Board members who were enthusiastic at the start have lost the sense of urgency for diversity outcomes in light of growing financial concerns of the organization. As with the prophet Elijah, we experienced a great victory, but the haters came out and we are tempted to say, "I have had enough, LORD" (1 Kings 19:4). This is when we can find comfort, not an excuse, in the phrase "progress, not perfection."

> Not that I have already obtained all this, or have already arrived at my goal, but I press on to take hold of that for which Christ Jesus took hold of me. Brothers and sisters, I do not consider myself yet to have taken hold of it. But one thing I do: Forgetting what is behind and straining toward what is ahead, I press on toward the goal to win the prize for which God has called me heavenward in Christ Jesus. (Phil. 3:12–14)

We long for perfection. We advance our cases for diversity to be and do better. We want change now—not next year or in ten years, but now. We, along with all of creation, groan for all relationships to be reconciled. As Christ followers, we know that sin has corrupted every individual, social system, and organization, even Christian organizations. Furthermore, we know that social systems and institutions will not be fully redeemed until the day of Christ's return. We will not be fully restored until the day of

Christ's return. So we live in this in-between space, the space between the now and the not yet, wondering if perfection will ever come, wondering if our labor is all in vain.

Your labor is *not* in vain. Let's say that one more time for the people in the back row. Your labor is not in vain. If the process and solutions for creating welcoming and inclusive organizations were simple, they would have been implemented long ago. If the work was easy, it would have been accomplished long ago. If the journey were short, it would have been completed long ago. The work of culture change is a marathon, not a sprint. We celebrate milestones knowing that there is more to do—much more to do. We pay tribute to the good work that has been done and plan for the next steps and the steps after that. We guard against resting on the accomplishments of that past. We guard against the distractions that would slow the work even more. We respect the process and our progress, knowing that in God's timing, all will be accomplished. He who began a good work will be faithful to complete it.

But lest we get too comfortable with not achieving goals but making progress, we want to share this sobering reminder from Sandra Upton, vice president of educational initiatives at the Cultural Intelligence Center: "Tangible progress or results can't be accomplished or sustained if inequitable systems aren't dismantled and individual behaviors don't change."[1] We have to be honest about the quality and state of our progress. If our goals are ambiguous, it's hard to honestly call anything progress—busyness, yes, but progress, no. If our goals are all the low-hanging fruit variety, it's hard to honestly say that we are making deep, meaningful, and pervasive change in the way that our organizations understand and practice diversity, inclusion, equity, and reconciliation. Though we may never achieve perfection, we should still aim for it. Though we may never achieve perfection, short of Christ's return, meaningful progress will happen when individual behaviors *and* systems change. Trying to change one without the other is counterproductive and ultimately ineffective.

---

[1]Dr. Sandra Upton, "The Case for Diversity: Social Justice or the Bottom Line," *Cultural Intelligence Center* (blog), May 14, 2018, https://culturalq.com/blog/the-case-for-diversity-social-justice-or-the-bottom-line/.

Signposts for the Journey

Signposts are visual, verbal, and written signs that provide information about current location and direction and distance to another location. When a person is on a long journey, signposts either affirm that the person is on the right path, or they alert the person to the fact that he or she is moving in the wrong direction. Signposts can also point out opportunities to pause, rest, and enjoy the view. Signposts are essential for a journey unless you intend to wander. Wandering around without a clear idea of where you are going or how long you will be wandering can be fun—if you are taking a walk in a park. Wandering while trying to launch or sustain diversity efforts results in false starts, poorly invested resources, and unsustainable efforts. Signposts are crucial for this work. Signposts are crucial for having an objective way of noting progress. The signposts we provide here are for you to identify your current location and offer examples of steps that could be taken to shift from where you are to where you want to be. This list is not exhaustive, but it is a start. For each statement below, ask yourself if the statement is mostly true, almost true, or not true at all.

- Diversity and inclusion have been formally identified as core values of our organization.
- Our organization understands the difference between diversity, inclusion, equity, and reconciliation.
- Our organization understands the difference between a business, social justice, and biblical case for diversity.
- Diversity goals, strategies, and outcomes have been formally identified and incorporated into a strategic action plan with measures of accountability.
- Our organizational leader regularly affirms the value of diversity, inclusion, equity, and reconciliation for both individuals and organizations.
- Diversity goals and strategies are vertically incorporated through the organization.
- Diversity goals and strategies are horizontally incorporated across organization departments.
- Members of our organization can articulate the value of diversity and state the organization's case for diversity.

- A statement of commitment to diversity is easily viewed and found on our organization's website and other official printed resources.
- Our diversity statement includes our commitment to valuing all persons—not addressing sexual orientation and gender expression—addressed in a formal document accessible to all that outlines our denominational/organizational stance (with biblical interpretation included).
- Compositional diversity is measured, reported on a regular basis, and can be accessed easily.
- Compositional diversity goals are in place and reflect the composition of our surrounding community.
- Members of our organization with marginalized identities feel valued and feel they are fully embraced as members of our organization.
- Members of our organization with privileged identities understand their privilege and seek to use it to advance diversity efforts.
- Changes in trends in compositional diversity are monitored.
- Turnover rates for marginalized members are equal to or below that of the majority members.
- Our organization has recruitment and retention objectives and a plan specifically for marginalized populations.
- Search committee members participate in antibias training (for each new search, and for both external and internal searches).
- Exit interviews are conducted consistently.
- Diversity-related professional development opportunities are offered regularly.
- Diversity-related professional development addresses several expressions of diversity.
- Participation in diversity-related professional development is required for promotion and retention.
- Our organization has a full-time chief diversity officer (an executive-level diversity professional).
- Our organization has a diversity committee or task force.
- Diversity efforts (training, resource development, assessments, support for marginalized members) are adequately funded to meet the need and be excellent.

- A diversity-focused climate survey has been conducted within the last two years.
- Equity gaps within our organization have been identified, and a plan has been implemented to close the gap.
- Members of the organization understand what constitutes bias, harassment, and discrimination.
- Our organization has a formal system in place to report bias, discrimination, and harassment.
- Members of our organization are confident that a report of bias, discrimination, or harassment will be taken seriously and resolved.
- Our organization is committed to transformation.
- Our organization strives for equity.
- Our organization is doing all it can do to achieve its diversity goals.
- Our organization has entrusted its diversity efforts to God and regularly prays for wisdom, understanding, perseverance, forgiveness, and success.

As you begin to engage the SHIFT process, an organic process of identifying signposts meaningful for your context and aligned with your mission will develop. Watch for them, adopt them, and act on them.

Bonus suggestion: have people from different parts of your organization complete this exercise or have members of your board of directors and community partners complete it as they reflect on what they believe to be true about your organization. I (Michelle L.) had both the executive leadership team and the diversity committee of my university complete a similar activity. The gap between the results of each group was eye opening. The gap signaled a need for better communication on the part of the diversity committee and a need for more engagement in diversity efforts by the executive leaders.

No True Progress without God

Strategic diversity plans are important for identifying the signposts of progress. We can accomplish goals, win awards for our work, and not have a single report of bias, discrimination, or harassment; but would that be considered success? For secular organizations, the answer would be *yes!* Of course. What else is there? If you are motivated by a business or social justice case for diversity, there is nothing else. However, for Christian organizations motivated by a biblical case for diversity, we believe there is more to success than accomplishing compositional goals and working through the SHIFT model. For we are reminded by Jesus in Matthew 16:26 that we can gain the whole world and yet lose our own souls. We are reminded by the story of Martha and Mary that while it is productive to be busy with doing good, we should not neglect the one needful thing of spending time with Jesus (Luke 10:38–42). And Psalm 127:1 is a reminder that our work apart from God is in vain: "Unless the LORD builds the house, the builders labor in vain. Unless the LORD watches over the city, the guards stand watch in vain."

As Christ followers, success involves the means *and* the ends, the outcomes and the method by which we accomplished results. In all that we do, we are implored to exhibit the fruit of the spirit of the Spirit: love, joy, peace, forbearance, kindness, goodness, faithfulness, gentleness, and self-control (Gal. 5:22–23). Internal and external forces may push and pull us into becoming more intentional about our diversity efforts, but it is the command to love our neighbors as ourselves that is our driving force. Assessments and signposts provide direction and awareness, but God provides wisdom. Policies and programs may change outward behavior, but it is the Holy Spirit who changes the heart. We do this work not for our own glory but that *God* may be glorified. That is the ultimate mark of success: God is glorified, and God's kingdom is advanced.

Takeaways

Signposts assure you that you either are on the right path and making progress or have strayed from the path and need to recalibrate. *Progress, not perfection.* Even the best organizations struggle with accomplishing diversity goals. In all we do, we must include God. Unless the Lord builds the house, we labor in vain.

CONCLUSION

> *But seek first his kingdom and his righteousness,*
> *and all these things will be given to you as well.*
> —Matthew 6:33

In her foreword to this book, Rev. Dr. Brenda Salter-McNeil calls our attention to the text in Matthew regarding new wine. She boldly exhorts that this is what is needed in Christian organizations. We agree! We need to talk a bit about imagination. It is vitally important that you are able to tap into the creative imagination of God. This work demands that we think outside the box. The challenges that face Christian organizations today are not the same challenges we wrestled with twenty years ago. Truthfully, they are different than they were a year ago.

While it is tempting to avoid controversial topics, we as Christ followers must be prepared to both celebrate the beauty of diversity and the challenges that arise when people challenge the status quo. To be clear, challenges to the status quo do not just come from the marginalized in our communities. We have only to look back at the video captures of recent protests to see that the faces in the crowds are usually multiracial and multigenerational. Congregants attending our churches, students attending our schools, and employees working in our businesses are being impacted by the social issues of our day—some, more than others. As Christ followers, we are called to engage the world that we may offer light in the darkness, healing for the hurting, and liberation for the captive. We cannot do these things if we are not willing to engage in difficult and uncomfortable conversation—with grace, truth, and humility. We must address LGBTQ+ concerns. We must address sexism and gender inequality. We must address all racial injustice and oppression. We must address White nationalism. But how do we have these conversations in ways that do not shame, wound, retrigger, humiliate, and ostracize the individuals we are called to serve? How do we serve both the marginalized and the privileged? How do we serve both those who are in denial of a need for social justice and those who are advocates for social justice? How do we celebrate the gains that have been made and keep pushing for change?

How? Well, we are still trying to figure this out. We do not have all the answers, but we know the One who does. We also know that business as usual will not bring personal or organizational transformation. The old ways are not enough (they would have worked by now if they were). We need new wine for this work, for this particular point in history. We need fresh ways to spread God's message of love to all humanity. We need to tap into the wellspring of the Spirit and allow that Living Water to flow. The Holy Spirit enables flourishing. With the help of the Spirit, there is no limit to what can be done within our personal lives and our organizations!

We would be remiss if we did not insert a word of caution regarding new wine. We are not suggesting that you throw out all your old methods for transforming hearts and organizations. There are some ways that may still work well. How will you know? Well, remember the transformation stage of the SHIFT model? Monitoring and assessing your efforts. Keep what is working. However, you may want to think of packaging or delivering your diversity efforts differently if they have not been modified or refreshed in a couple of years.

For instance, storytelling is one of the most powerful tools in our work. Stories break down resistance, build empathy, and push past superficiality in a way that nothing else can. In the words of Tyrion from *Game of Thrones*, "What unites people? Armies? Gold? Flags? STORIES! There's nothing in the world more powerful than a good story. Nothing can stop it. No enemy can defeat it."

So how do we reimagine storytelling? Simply by utilizing the technology at our fingertips through social media and videos to tell our stories. Telling stories through the arts is incredibly effective. Becoming proficient storytellers involves adaptation. Adaptation involves imagination.

The Ultimate Goal Is Reconciliation

Ultimately, the Christian organizations where we work are not ours. We may be fixtures. We may have poured our lives in these organizations. We may have even sacrificed much and endured much, but shedding tears and staying up late do not give us ownership. Our organizations—every worker, every client, every student, every program—belong to God. The work belongs to God. *We* belong to God! Let that free your mind and your time. It doesn't all rest on the shoulders of any one of us (even though it feels like it at times).

> Therefore, if anyone is in Christ, the new creation has come: The old has gone, the new is here! All this is from God, who reconciled us to himself through Christ and gave us the ministry of reconciliation: that God was reconciling the world to himself in Christ, not counting people's sins against them. And he has committed to us the message of reconciliation. (2 Cor. 5:17–19)

We have been given this ministry. God has committed it to us, but it is *from God*. This work comes from God's heart and fills ours. In our experience, diversity work is a ministry, a matter of the heart, with an eye toward the reconciliation of all things. The reconciliation of all things requires the transformation of all things: people, churches, schools, businesses, cities, nations, and ourselves. Diversity professionals are in the transformation business. Outliers, allies, and co-conspirators are in the transformation business. Christian organizations are in the transformation business. We are called to assist in changing hearts and broadening minds. We are called to help people think and love like Jesus. Systems do not change without a transformation. Jesus came in and upended an entire system with his message of love and redemption.

For many in this work, the word *reconciliation* has been considered a weak term lacking "justice teeth" and allowing Christians to engage in watered-down attempts to address societal divides. We contend that compositional diversity + inclusion + equity + faith = reconciliation. It is our belief that you cannot have reconciliation until you address issues of compositional diversity, equitable treatment, inclusive practices, and the belief that God is in all and above all. We acknowledge that reconciliation is easier to pray about than to do. But reconciliation is not a creation of the human mind; it is a command that flows from God's heart. That is why reconciliation is the ultimate goal.

Some Parting Thoughts (Michelle L.)

"Now to him who is able to do immeasurably more than all we ask or imagine, according to his power that is at work within us, to him be glory in the church and in Christ Jesus throughout all generations, for ever and ever! Amen" (Eph. 3:20–21). My diversity-professional journey has been one adventurous ride. I have had days when I wanted to call it quits and return to my grad-school job of cashiering at a grocery store. I have had days where a person drops by my office unexpectedly to say thank you for helping her better understand microaggressions. I have designed workshops for which only one person showed up and I have designed workshops in which one-hundred people were fully engaged (I know because I read the evaluations). In short, I have had good days, and I have had bad days, and as the gospel song says, "I won't complain." I have been a diversity professional for over thirty years. My skills were honed in the classroom as a faculty member, refined as a dean, polished as a senior executive, and expanded as a consultant to nonprofit organizations and health-care systems. However, I know that the work that I do—the good, the setbacks, the progress, and the frustrations—is all a part of God's good work and plan. My desire for a welcoming and diverse campus is nothing compared to God's heart for my campus. My longing for welcoming and diverse nonprofit organizations and churches pales in comparison to God's heart for organizations that call themselves by God's name. For any diversity effort to be successful, it must start with God's heart.

Are there days when you feel inadequate, when you wonder if the needle will ever move—even an inch? Great! Welcome to the club. You are now positioned to realize that change will come not just from your efforts or the efforts of your team—change will come because God is at work. God is weaving the chaotic threads of change into a beautiful diversity tapestry. That's good news; and even better is the knowledge that God can do even more than we can think and ask.

I have found great comfort in realizing that God knows better than I do and can do much, much more than I can do. My job is to lean into God's plans, listen for God's direction, and trust the process on the way to the outcome. I can't do everything that needs to be done—actually, I can't even *think* of everything that needs to be done. I have learned to trust my campus to God and to align my heart with God's.

Some Parting Thoughts (Michelle W.)

I didn't set out to become a diversity professional. I set out to be obedient to God. I answered a call. I wanted to have maximum impact. God decided to place me within a local church body and within Christian higher education. Along the way, I've been deeply disappointed and have seen glimpses of glory. Who am I to judge God's people who are in process? After all, I am one of those people. All I can do is continue to try building bridges that connect people to each other and to the heart of God. God calls us to love one another. My job is to join in with God's reconciling love mission. I am an ambassador of reconciliation.

One of my favorite quotes is by noted theorist Jean Baker Miller: "We all want to feel 'seen, heard, and understood.'" This is the foundation of all human interaction for me. The only way to promote open communication and trust is to see individuals as possessing the same human dignity as you; to value their voices and listen when they speak; and to seek to understand their perspective, even if it is different than your own.

I believe listening is a lost art. With the advent of social media, people have become accustomed to shouting at one another through a fairly anonymous, disconnected platform. Over the years, I've tried to cultivate the art of listening well. I repeat two simple mantras before any difficult conversations. The first is a fundamental truth meant to align my perspective with God's perspective (and therefore silence my biases). Here it is: "This person is made in the image of God. Therefore, they are worthy of my love and respect. No matter who they are, no matter what they've done, God loves them and commands me to do the same."

The second one is similar yet helps me in a different way. It gives me an internal "checklist." I mentioned it above, but it bears repeating. "We all want to feel 'seen, heard, and understood.'" At the end of a difficult conversation, I go back and ask myself, "How did I demonstrate that I saw, heard, and understood that individual?"

Listening well is hard and holy work. As Diana Senechal says, "Listening involves a certain *surrender*, a willingness to sit with what one does not already know. . . . Listening requires us to stretch a little beyond what we know, expect, or want."

Finally, I would like to speak to the issue of mutual need and mutual benefit. The need for competent, caring, discerning diversity professionals in Christian organizations is evident. The need for humble, vocal, and consistently aspiring allies and co-conspirators is equally evident. The overarching need for inclusive, caring, and teachable organizations is evident as well. These needs are not exclusive. If you have one without any of the others, then the goal of creating a reconciled, kingdom-centered organization will not be met.

Takeaways

Instead of summarizing, we wanted to leave you with a list of questions. We believe this work is transformational. For transformation to occur in our organizations, it must begin in the individual. Below you will find two lists. One addresses personal transformation and the other addresses the organizational transformation. We believe in the healing power of community. We invite you to connect with members of your community and discuss the questions below.

Personal Transformation Questions

1. How would you describe your calling to this work?
   a. Is it one that fills you with hope and joy—or fear and dread?

b. What excites you most about your calling?

2. How are you doing in this role?
    a. What have you learned about yourself?
    b. What is the state of your mental and physical health?
    c. What have you learned about your leadership skills?

3. Who are you becoming in this process?
    a. What have you learned about your capacity for forgiveness?
    b. What have you learned about your need for healing and redemption?

Organizational Transformation Questions

1. Where would you place your organization within the SHIFT model?
    a. What informs this placement?
    b. Are you pleased with this placement? Surprised? Saddened?

2. How does your organization know it has been successful?
    a. Are there diversity-related goals within the strategic plan?
    b. How is success defined?
    c. How often are goals reviewed?

Finally, please know that you are not in this alone. We'd love to hear your answers to these questions and provide space for dialogue. We can be reached at www.diversity-playbook.com. We'd love to engage with you further.

NOW IS THE TIME

> *Start where you are. Use what you have. Do what you can.*
> —Arthur Ashe
>
> *If not you, then who? If not now, then when?*
> —Rabbi Hillel

Right about now, whether you've read the whole book or just the part that you felt most directly corresponded to your most pressing concern, you're likely feeling a bit overwhelmed. We presented a lot of information, and yet there is no way we could cover every relevant topic and every possible scenario. And as we have said before, some things just have to be experienced. Right about now, you may be thinking, "Okay— you convinced me. I want to make the move from being an outlier to a co-conspirator," or "I want to lead my organization from just celebrating diversity to enacting equity, but how and when do I start the process?" *When?* and *How?* are the million-dollar questions. And our million-dollar answer is *Now is the time*.

We can already hear the *yeah, buts*—"Yeah, but I'm only one person." "Yeah, but my organization doesn't have a diversity budget or the budget was cut in half last year." "Yeah, but my organization doesn't have a diversity statement, let alone a strategic diversity plan." Yeah, but I have only one ally." "Yeah, but my organization doesn't have compositional diversity." We get the *yeah, buts*. We have thought and uttered our own many times. However, don't let them prevent you from starting where you are, using what you have, and doing what you can do now—with or without a budget, with or without the confidence that everything you put your hands to do will prosper. Just start. Take the next step and trust that God will guide your next step . . . and the next . . . and the one after that. Believe that he who began the good work of diversity, inclusion, equity, and reconciliation in you and your organization will be faithful to see it to completion (Phil. 1:6). We are not in this work alone. God is with us. After all, if God is not a part of our efforts, we labor in vain (Ps. 127:1). We believe that God's commandments to love our neighbors, to act justly, and to love mercy should be evident in our daily interactions with those around us and within the fabric of our organizations. A tall order—maybe even impossible if we rely only on our own strength—but we are assured in God's Word that what is impossible with us is possible with God (Luke 18:27). Blessings on your journey and as you begin or continue this good work. Remember to ground it in prayer.

A Prayer and Blessing for Your Journey

Creator God,

We bless your name. You are holy and righteous. The breadth of your love for us is incomprehensible. While we were yet sinners and estranged from you, you still loved us and pursued us. As we learned to accept your love, our hearts began to align with yours.

Because you are love, you have called us to love the stranger, to love our enemies, to love justice and mercy. But we have failed to love as deeply as you love and we have failed to love what you love. Help us, heal us, forgive us, and correct us.

Transform our hearts and minds. Call us to a deeper love, a love that builds rather than destroys, a love that gathers together rather than pulls apart, a love that gives rather than takes. You have shown us what deep love is. Love is patient and kind. It does not dishonor others It always protects, always trusts, always hopes, and always preserves. Deepen our capacity to love our neighbors as you love them.

Transform our organizations and our communities. May they become known as agents of renewal, known to celebrate diversity and inclusion, known to champion equity, and known to act justly. We acknowledge that we cannot do this work without you and that we cannot be successful unless all we do is committed to building your kingdom.

Realign our mission, our vision, our values, and our practices. May the places where we lead, work, learn, and worship more genuinely reflect the kingdom and foster shalom.

In Christ's name we pray.
Amen.

Now to him who is able to do immeasurably more than all we ask or imagine, according to his power that is at work within us, to him be glory in the church and in Christ Jesus throughout all generations, for ever and ever! Amen. (Eph. 3:20–21)

Let's Connect

We would love to continue the conversation with you. We've provided a space for dialogue, questions, and engagement here:

www.diversity-playbook.com

Michelle R. Loyd-Paige   Michelle D. Williams

DIVERSITY MATTERS

Race, Ethnicity, & the Future of Christian Higher Education

Allison N. Ash, Alexander Jun, Kathy-Ann Hernandez,
Rebecca Hernandez, Michelle Loyd-Paige, & Pete Menjares, Section Editors

Karen A. Longman, General Editor

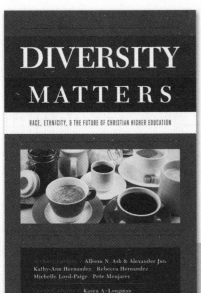

ISBN: 978-0-89112-454-2

Today, no institution can ignore the need for deep conversations about race and ethnicity. But colleges and universities face a unique set of challenges as they explore these topics. *Diversity Matters* offers leaders a roadmap as they think through how their campuses can serve all students well. Each chapter includes important discussion questions for administration, faculty, and staff.

"*Diversity Matters is a welcome offering not just in the realm of evangelical Christian higher education, but also in the realm of evangelical Christianity as a whole. Through it, the contributors clearly and courageously address the why, the what, and the how of developing institutions where racial and ethnic diversity can flourish in ways that benefit the institutions and honor God.*"

—Bishop Claude Alexander, pastor of The Park Church, Charlotte, NC

"*We are at a critical moment in Christian education in regard to diversity. With the demographics of our nation changing dramatically every year, it is imperative that the church and Christian institutions of higher learning keep pace with this changing reality. To that end, Diversity Matters offers sound advice to all who wish to join in this necessary progress.*"

—Noel Castellanos, President, Camino Alliance

1-877-816-4455 toll free
www.acupressbooks.com

Abilene Christian University Press